OTHER WORKS BY MAYA ANGELOU:

*And Still I Rise*
*Gather Together in My Name*
*The Heart of a Woman*
*I Know Why the Caged Bird Sings*
*Just Give Me A Cool Drink of Water 'Fore I Diiie*
*Oh Pray My Wings Are Gonna Fit Me Well*
*Singin' and Swingin' and Gettin' Merry Like Christmas*
*Shaker, Why Don't You Sing?*

# All God's Children Need Traveling Shoes

# All God's Children Need Traveling Shoes

MAYA ANGELOU

RANDOM HOUSE / NEW YORK

All rights reserved under International and Pan-American
Copyright Conventions. Published in the United States by
Random House, Inc., New York and simultaneously in Canada by
Random House of Canada Limited, Toronto.

Library of Congress Cataloging-in-Publication Data

Angelou, Maya.
All God's children need traveling shoes.

Autobiography.
1. Angelou, Maya—Biography.   2. Authors, American—
20th century—Biography.   3. Entertainers—United
States—Biography.   I. Title.
PS3551.N464Z463   1986      818'.5409   [B]        85-19351
ISBN 0-394-52143-9

A signed first edition of this book has been privately printed
by The Franklin Library

Manufactured in the United States of America

68975

This book is dedicated to
Julian and Malcolm and all the fallen ones
who were passionately and earnestly
looking for a home.

Swing Low, Sweet Chariot,
Coming for to carry me home.

## ACKNOWLEDGMENTS

A special thank you to Ruben Medina and Alan Palmer for their brotherly love and laughter through many years. Thanks to Jean and Roger Genoud for their camaraderie during our strange and rich years, to Seymour Lazar for belief in my youthful ambition, and to Shana Alexander for talking to me about the mystery of return. Thanks to Anna Budu-Arthur for being a constant Sister.

# All God's Children Need Traveling Shoes

The breezes of the West African night were intimate and shy, licking the hair, sweeping through cotton dresses with unseemly intimacy, then disappearing into the utter blackness. Daylight was equally insistent, but much more bold and thoughtless. It dazzled, muddling the sight. It forced through my closed eyelids, bringing me up and out of a borrowed bed and into brand new streets.

After living nearly two years in Cairo, I had brought my son Guy to enter the University of Ghana in Accra. I planned staying for two weeks with a friend of a colleague, settling Guy into his dormitory, then continuing to Liberia to a job with the Department of Information.

Guy was seventeen and quick. I was thirty-three and determined. We were Black Americans in West Africa, where for the first time in our lives the color of our skin was accepted as correct and normal.

Guy had finished high school in Egypt, his Arabic was good and his health excellent. He assured me that he would quickly learn a Ghanaian language, and he certainly could look after himself. I had worked successfully as a journalist in Cairo, and failed sadly at a marriage which I ended with false public dignity and copious secret tears. But with all crying in the past, I was on my way to another adventure. The future was plump with promise.

For two days Guy and I laughed. We looked at the Ghanaian streets and laughed. We listened to the melodious languages and laughed. We looked at each other and laughed out loud.

On the third day, Guy, on a pleasure outing, was injured in an automobile accident. One arm and one leg were fractured and his neck was broken.

July and August of 1962 stretched out like fat men yawning after a sumptuous dinner. They had every right to gloat, for they had eaten me up. Gobbled me down. Consumed my spirit, not in a wild rush, but slowly, with the obscene patience of certain victors. I became a shadow walking in the white hot streets, and a dark spectre in the hospital.

There was no solace in knowing that the doctors and nurses hovering around Guy were African, nor in the company of the Black American expatriates who, hearing of our misfortune, came to share some of the slow hours. Racial loyalties and cultural attachments had become meaningless.

Trying utterly, I could not match Guy's stoicism. He lay calm, week after week, in a prison of plaster from which only his face and one leg and arm were visible. His assurances that he would heal and be better than new drove me into a faithless silence. Had I been less timid, I would have cursed God. Had I come from a different background, I would have gone further and denied His very existence. Having neither the courage nor the historical precedent, I raged inside myself like a blinded bull in a metal stall.

Admittedly, Guy lived with the knowledge that an unexpected and very hard sneeze could force the fractured vertebrae against his spinal cord, and he would be paralyzed or die immediately, but he had only an infatuation with life. He hadn't lived long enough to fall in love with this brutally delicious experience. He could lightly waft away to another place, if there really was another place, where his youthful innocence would assure him a crown, wings, a harp, ambrosia, free milk and an absence of nostalgic yearning. (I was raised on the spirituals which ached to "See my old mother in glory" or "Meet with my dear children in heaven," but even the most fanciful lyricists never dared to suggest that those cavorting souls gave one thought to those of us left to moil in the world.) My wretchedness reminded me that, on the other hand, I would be rudderless.

I had lived with family until my son was born in my sixteenth year. When he was two months old and perched on my left hip, we left my mother's house and together, save for one year when I was touring, we had been each other's home and center for seventeen years. He could die if he wanted to and go off to wherever dead folks go, but I, I would be left without a home.

The man who caused the accident stood swaying at the foot of the bed. Drunk again, or, two months later, still drunk. He, the host of the motor trip and the owner of the car, had passed out on the back seat leaving Guy behind the steering wheel trying to start the stalled engine. A truck had careened off a steep hill and plowed into Richard's car, and he had walked away unhurt.

Now he dangled loosely in the room, looking shyly at me. "Hello, Sister Maya." The slurred words made me hate him more. My whole body yearned for his scrawny neck. I turned my face from the scoundrel and looked at my son. The once white plaster that encased his body and curved around his face was yellowing and had begun to crumble.

I spoke softly, as people do to the very old, the very young, and the sick. "Darling, how are you today?"

"Mother, Richard spoke to you." His already deep voice growled with disapproval.

"Hello, Richard," I mumbled, hoping he couldn't hear me.

My greeting penetrated the alcoholic fog, and the man lumbered into an apologetic monologue that tested my control. "I'm sorry, Sister Maya. So sorry. If only it could be me, there on that bed ... Oh, if only it could be me ..."

I agreed with him.

At last he had done with his regrets, and saying good-bye to Guy, took my hand. Although his touch was repulsive, Guy was watching me, so I placed a silly grin on my face and said, "Good-bye, Richard." After he left, I began quickly to unload the basket of food I had brought. (The teenage appetite is not thwarted by bruises or even broken bones.)

Guy's voice stopped me.

"Mother, come so I can see you."

The cast prevented him from turning, so visitors had to stand directly in his vision. I put the basket down and went to stand at the foot of the bed.

His face was clouded with anger.

"Mother, I know I'm your only child, but you must remember, this is my life, not yours." The thorn from the bush one has planted, nourished and pruned, pricks most deeply and draws more blood. I waited in agony as he continued, eyes scornful and lips curled, "If I can see Richard and understand that he has been more hurt than I, what about you? Didn't you mean all those sermons about tolerance? All that stuff about understanding? About before you criticize a man, you should walk a mile in his shoes?"

Of course I meant it in theory, in conversation about the underprivileged, misunderstood and oppressed miscreants, but not about a brute who had endangered my son's life.

I lied and said, "Yes, I meant it." Guy smiled and said, "I know you did, Mother. You're just upset now." His face framed by the cast was beautiful with forgiveness. "Don't worry anymore. I'm going to get out of here soon, then you can go on to Liberia."

I made bitterness into a wad and swallowed it.

I puckered and grinned and said, "You're right, darling. I won't be upset anymore."

As always, we found something to laugh about. He fumbled, eating with his unbroken left hand and when he did have the food firmly in his grasp, he pretended not to know how to find his mouth. Crumbs littered his gown. "I'll figure it out, Mom. I promise you I won't starve to death." We played word games, and the visiting hours went by quickly.

Too soon I was back on the bright street with an empty basket in my hands and my head swimming in the lonely air.

I did know some people who would receive me, but reluctantly, because I had nothing to offer company save a long face and a self-pitying heart, and I had no intention of changing either. Black Americans of my generation didn't look kindly on public mournings except during or immediately after funerals. We were expected by others and by ourselves to lighten the burden by smiling, to deflect possible new assaults by laughter. Hadn't it worked for us for centuries? Hadn't it?

On our first night in Ghana, our host (who was only a friend of a friend) invited Black American and South American expatriates to meet us. Julian Mayfield and his beautiful wife Ana Livia, who was a medical doctor, were known to me from New York and the rest were not. But there is a kinship among wanderers, as operative as the bond between bishops or the tie between thieves: We knew each other instantly and exchanged anecdotes, contacts and even addresses within the first hour.

Alice Windom, a wit from St. Louis, and Vicki Garvin, a gentle woman from New York City, were among the Americans laughing and entertaining in the small living room. In the two years which had passed since Guy had been in the company of so many Black Americans, he had grown from a precocious adolescent into an adept young man. He bristled with pleasure, discovering that he could hold his own in the bantering company.

Each émigré praised Ghana and questioned my plans to settle in Liberia. There was no need to tell them that I hungered for security and would have accepted nearly any promised permanence in Africa. They knew, but kept up the teasing. One asked, "You remember that Ray Charles song where he says, 'When you leave New York, you ain't going nowhere'?"

I remembered.

"Well, when you leave Ghana, going to Liberia, you ain't going to Africa, in fact you ain't going nowhere."

Although I knew Liberians who were as African as Congo drums, I honored the traditional procedure and allowed the raillery to continue.

Alice advised, "Honey, you'd better stay here, get a job and settle down. It can't get better than Ghana and it could be a lot worse." Everyone laughed and agreed.

The fast talk and jokes were packages from home and I was delighted to show the group that I still knew how to act in Black company. I laughed as hard as the teasers and enjoyed the camaraderie.

But Guy's accident erased all traces of their names, their faces and conviviality. I felt as if I had met no one, knew no one, and had lived my entire life as the bereft mother of a seriously injured child.

Tragedy, no matter how sad, becomes boring to those not caught in its addictive caress. I watched my host, so sympathetic at the outset, become increasingly less interested in me and my distress. After a few weeks in his house, his discomfort even penetrated my self-centeredness. When Julian and Ana Livia Mayfield allowed me to store my books and clothes at their house, I gave my host only perfunctory thanks, and moved into a tiny room at the local YWCA I focused my attention on myself, with occasional concentrations on Guy. If I thought about it I was relieved that no one anticipated my company, yet, I took the idea of rejection as one more ornament on my string of worry beads.

One sunny morning Julian stood waiting for me in the YWCA lobby. His good looks drew attention and giggles from the young women who sat on the vinyl chairs pretending to read.

"I'm taking you to meet someone. Someone you should know." He looked at me without smiling. He was tall, Black, tough and brusque.

"You need to have someone, a woman, talk to you. Let's go." I withdrew from his proprietary air, but lack of energy prevented me from telling him that he wasn't my brother, he wasn't even a close friend. For want of resistance, I followed him to his car.

"Somebody needs to tell you that you have to give up this self-pity. You're letting yourself go. Look at your clothes. Look at your hair. Hell, it's Guy whose neck was broken. Not yours."

Anger jumped up in my mouth, but I held back the scorching words and turned to look at him. He was watching the road, but the side of his face visible to me was tense, his eyes were unblinking, and he had pushed his full lips out in a pout.

"Everybody understands ... as much as anyone can understand another's pain ... but you've ... you've forgotten to be polite. Hell, girl, everybody feels sorry for you, but nobody owes you a damn thing. You know that. Don't forget your background. Your mother didn't raise you in a dog house."

Blacks concede that hurrawing, jibing, jiving, signifying, disrespecting, cursing, even outright insults might be acceptable under particular conditions, but aspersions cast against one's family call for immediate attack.

I said, "How do you know my business so well? Was that my daddy visiting your mother all those times he left our home?"

I expected an explosion from Julian. Yet his response shocked me. Laughter burst out of him, loud and raucous. The car wobbled and slowed while he held tenuously to the steering wheel. I caught his laughter, and it made me pull his jacket, and slap my own knee. Miraculously we stayed on the road. We were still laughing when he pulled into a driveway and let the engine die.

"Girl, you're going to be all right. You haven't forgotten the essentials. You know about defending yourself. All you have to do now is remember . . . sometimes you have to defend yourself from yourself."

When we got out of the car Julian hugged me and we walked together toward The National Theatre of Ghana, a round, white building set in an embrace of green-black trees.

Efua Sutherland could have posed for the original bust of Nefertiti. She was long, lean, Black and lovely, and spoke so softly I had to lean forward to catch her words. She wore an impervious air as obvious as a strong perfume, and an austere white floor-length gown.

She sat motionless as Julian recounted my dreadful tale and ended saying that my only child was, even as we spoke, in the Military Hospital. When Julian stopped talking and looked at her pointedly, I was pleased that Efua's serene face did not crumble into pity. She was silent and Julian continued. "Maya is a writer. We knew each other at home. She worked for Martin Luther King. She's pretty much alone here, so I have to be a brother to her, but she needs to talk to a woman, and pretty soon she'll need a job." Efua said nothing, but finally turned to me and I had the feeling that all of myself was being absorbed. The moment was long.

"Maya," she stood and walked to me. "Sister Maya, we will see about a job, but now you have need of a Sister friend." I had not cried since the accident. I had helped to lift Guy's inert body onto the x-ray table at the first hospital, had assisted in carrying his stretcher to an ambulance for transfer to another hospital. I had slept, awakened, walked, and lived in a thick atmosphere, which only allowed shallow breathing and routine motor behavior.

Efua put her hand on my cheek and repeated, "Sister, you have need of a Sister friend because you need to weep, and you need someone to watch you while you weep." Her gestures and voice were mesmerizing. I began to cry. She stroked my face for a minute then returned to her chair. She began speaking to Julian about other matters. I continued crying and was embarrassed when I couldn't stop the tears. When I was a child, my grandmother would observe me weeping and say, "Be careful, Sister. The more you cry, the less you'll pee, and peeing is more important." But the faucet, once opened, had to drain itself. I had no power over its flow.

Efua sent Julian away with assurances that she would return me to the hospital. I looked at her, but she had settled into herself sweetly, and I was freed to cry out all the bitterness and self-pity of the past days.

When I had finished, she stood again, offering me a handkerchief. "Now, Sister, you must eat. Eat and drink. Replenish yourself." She called her chauffeur, and we were taken to her home.

She was a poet, playwright, teacher, and the head of Ghana's National Theatre. We talked in the car of Shakespeare, Langston Hughes, Alexander Pope and Sheridan. We agreed that art was the flower of life and despite the years of ill-treatment Black artists were among its most glorious blossoms.

She knew the president and called him familiarly "Kwame."

She said, "Kwame has said that Ghana must use its own legends to heal itself. I have written the old tales in new ways to teach the children that their history is rich and noble."

Her house, white as chalk and stark, had rounded walls which enclosed a green lawn. Her three children came laughing to greet me, and her servant brought me food. Efua spoke in Fanti to the maid, and a mixture of Fanti and English to the children.

"This is your Auntie Maya. She shall be coming frequently. Her son is ill, but you shall meet him, for he will soon be released from the hospital."

Esi Rieter, the oldest, a girl of ten, Ralph, seven, and the five-year-old, Amowi, immediately wanted to know how old my son was, what was his illness, did I have other children, what did I do. Efua sent them away assuring them that time would answer all questions.

I ate as I had cried, generously. After the meal, Efua walked me to the car.

"Sister, you are not alone. I, myself, will be at the hospital tomorrow. Your son is now my son. He has two mothers in this place." She put her hand on my face again. "Sister, exercise patience. Try."

When the driver stopped at the hospital, I felt cool and refreshed as if I had just gone swimming in Bethesda's pool, and many of my cares had been washed away in its healing water.

The hospital acquired color, there was laughter in its halls and Guy's good humor stopped being contrived. He and the doctors, surprisingly, had been right. Recovery was evident in the ways of his hands and in his lumbering, cast-top-heavy lurching up and down the corridors.

Outside, the sun, which had pounced, penetrating and hostile, now covered me with beneficial rays, hoisting me out of depression and back on my feet, where my new mood told me I deserved to be.

I smiled at strangers and took notice of buildings and streets. Weeks passed before I was conscious that I had let go of misery.

The visit to Efua, and Julian's reluctant but sincere offer to be my brother had been very strong medicine.

I was impatient to get my life in order. Obviously, I wouldn't go to Liberia, so . . . I had to find a job, a car and a house for Guy to come to while he continued recuperating. I needed to get my hair cut, a manicure, a pedicure. My clothes were disgraceful.

Flashes of panic occurred and recurred. Was it possible that during the two-month depression, I had damaged my determination? The only power I had ever claimed was that I had over myself. Obviously, I had come perilously close to giving it away to self-pity.

I thought about Julian's hard words, "Your mother didn't raise you in a dog house." His intuition had come understated.

My mother, that pretty little woman with a steel chest, had taught me and my brother Bailey that each person was expected to "paddle his own canoe, stand on his own feet, put his own shoulder to the wheel, and work like hell." She always added, "Hope for the best, but be prepared for the worst. You may not always get what you pay for, but you will definitely pay for what you get." Vivian Baxter had axioms for every situation, and if one didn't come to mind when she needed it, she would create a better one on the moment.

I had been a pretty good student, ingesting and internalizing her advice, so now I pushed away the gnawing fear that I might have lost some of my vital willfulness.

I looked at the disheveled mess I had been living in and at my nearby neighbors. To my surprise, many of the women who had been at that first-night party and who had faithfully attended Guy's hospital room, lived down the hall from me. I was also amazed to learn that mops, brooms, pails and other cleaning implements were available for the free use of the center's guests.

Alice and Vicki watched me emerge from the bonds of my chrysalis and accepted me with no comment, save an easy teasing. While I swabbed my small floor and washed my clothes Alice said, "I would offer to help you Maya, but somehow I didn't inherit any of the race's domestic talents."

Vicki offered, but I knew the work was cathartic, so I washed walls, polished door knobs and the tiny window. The scales and stench of defeat floated into the pail's dirty water.

The YWCA residents forgave me my drunken spree with hopelessness and we began to spend time together in the building's cafeteria and on the streets filled with views I had not seen. Alice took me to Black Star Square to see the monumental arch, named in part for the newspaper founded in the United States by the ex-slave and abolitionist, Frederick Douglass.

Vicki and Sylvia Boone rode with me to Flagstaff House, the seat of government. Seeing Africans enter and leave the formal building made me tremble with an awe I had never known. Their authority on the marble steps again proved that Whites had been wrong all along. Black and brown skin did not herald debasement and a divinely created inferiority. We were capable of controlling our cities, our selves and our lives with elegance and success. Whites were not needed to explain the working of the world, nor the mysteries of the mind.

My visits to the hospital diminished to one daily appearance and Guy's gladness made me young again.

Efua introduced me to the chairman of the Institute of African Studies at the university and pleaded with him to hire me. She had told him that I had been on my way to a job in Liberia until my seventeen-year-old son had been involved in an accident, adding that I had to stay in Ghana until he fully recovered. She smiled at him and said I was already trying to hear Fanti, and would make a good Ghanaian.

Professor J. H. Nketia, one of Ghana's leading scholars, was so unpretentious as to be unsettling. He listened with patience to Efua, then asked me, "Can you type?" When I said only a little, but that I could file and write, he gathered his chin in a stubby brown hand and smiled. "Can you start on Monday?" He told me I would be paid on the Ghanaian scale and he would arrange for me to get a small car. I knew that the proffered job spoke more of his own compassion and his affection for Efua than of a need for my services.

Foreign employees at the university earned high salaries, compared to the national average wage, and very liberal compensations. They were given housing allowances, tuition or aid for their offspring's education, transportation allowances and a perk charmingly referred to as dislocation allowance. They had been recruited in their own countries, and hired for their academic credentials and experience. Save for two youthful years at night school, I had only a high school education.

I challenged myself to do whatever job assigned to me with intense commitment and a good cheerfulness.

A professor went on leave and I moved into his house for three months. When Guy was released from the hospital he settled into our furnished, if temporary, home.

The community of Black immigrants opened and fitted me into their lives as if they had been saving my place.

The group's leader, if such a collection of eccentric egos could be led, was Julian. He had three books published in the United States, had acted in a Broadway play, and was a respected American-based intellectual before an encounter with the CIA and the FBI caused him to flee his country for Africa. He was accompanied in flight and supported, in fact, by Ana Livia, who was at least as politically volatile as he.

Sylvia Boone, a young sociologist, had come to Africa first on a church affiliated tour, then returned with sophistication, a second Master's degree and fluent French to find her place on the Continent. Ted Pointiflet was a painter who argued gently, but persistently that Africa was the inevitable destination of all Black Americans. Lesley Lacy, a sleek graduate student, was an expert on Marxism and Garveyism, while Jim and Annette Lacy, no relation to Lesley, were grade school teachers and quite rare among our group because they listened more than they talked. The somber faced Frank Robinson, a plumber, had a contagious laughter, and a fierce devotion to Nkrumah. Vicki Garvin had been a union organizer, Alice Windom had been trained in sociology. I called the group "Revolutionist Returnees."

Each person had brought to Africa varying talents, energies, vigor, youth and terrible yearnings to be accepted. On Julian's side porch during warm black nights, our voices were raised in attempts to best each other in lambasting America and extolling Africa.

We drank gin and ginger ale when we could afford it, and Club beer when our money was short. We did not discuss the open gutters along the streets of Accra, the shacks of corrugated iron in certain neighborhoods, dirty beaches and voracious mosquitoes. And under no circumstances did we mention our disillusionment at being overlooked by the Ghanaians.

We had come home, and if home was not what we had expected, never mind, our need for belonging allowed us to ignore the obvious and to create real places or even illusory places, befitting our imagination.

Doctors were in demand, so Ana Livia had been quickly placed in the Military Hospital and within a year, had set up a woman's clinic where she and her platoon of nursing sisters treated up to two hundred women daily. Progressive journalists were sought after, so Julian, who wrote articles for American and African journals, also worked for the *Ghana Evening News*. Frank and his partner Carlos Allston from Los Angeles founded a plumbing and electric company. Their success gave heart to the rest. We had little doubt about our likability. After the Africans got to know us their liking would swiftly follow. We didn't question if we would be useful. Our people for over three hundred years had been made so useful, a bloody war had been fought and lost, rather than have our usefulness brought to an end. Since we were descendants of African slaves torn from the land, we reasoned we wouldn't have to earn the right to return, yet we wouldn't be so arrogant as to take anything for granted. We would work and produce, then snuggle down into Africa as a baby nuzzles in a mother's arms.

I was soon swept into an adoration for Ghana as a young girl falls in love, heedless and with slight chance of finding the emotion requited.

There was an obvious justification for my amorous feelings. Our people had always longed for home. For centuries we had sung about a place not built with hands, where the streets were paved with gold, and were washed with honey and milk. There the saints would march around wearing white robes and jeweled crowns. There, at last, we would study war no more and, more important, no one would wage war against us again.

The old Black deacons, ushers, mothers of the church and junior choirs only partially meant heaven as that desired destination. In the yearning, heaven and Africa were inextricably combined.

And now, less than one hundred years after slavery was abolished, some descendants of those early slaves taken from Africa, returned, weighted with a heavy hope, to a continent which they could not remember, to a home which had shamefully little memory of them.

Which one of us could know that years of bondage, brutalities, the mixture of other bloods, customs and languages had transformed us into an unrecognizable tribe? Of course, we knew that we were mostly unwanted in the land of our birth and saw promise on our ancestral continent.

I was in Ghana by accident, literally, but the other immigrants had chosen the country because of its progressive posture and its brilliant president, Kwame Nkrumah. He had let it be known that American Negroes would be welcome to Ghana. He offered havens for Southern and East African revolutionaries working to end colonialism in their countries.

I admitted that while Ghana's domestic and foreign policy were stimulating, I was captured by the Ghanaian people. Their skins were the colors of my childhood cravings: peanut butter, licorice, chocolate and caramel. Theirs was the laughter of home, quick and without arti-

fice. The erect and graceful walk of the women reminded
me of my Arkansas grandmother, Sunday-hatted, on her
way to church. I listened to men talk, and whether or not I
understood their meaning, there was a melody as familiar
as sweet potato pie, reminding me of my Uncle Tommy
Baxter in Santa Monica, California. So I had finally come
home. The prodigal child, having strayed, been stolen or
sold from the land of her fathers, having squandered her
mother's gifts and having laid down in cruel gutters, had
at last arisen and directed herself back to the welcoming
arms of the family where she would be bathed, clothed
with fine raiment and seated at the welcoming table.

I was one of nearly two hundred Black Americans from
St. Louis, New York City, Washington, D.C., Los Angeles,
Atlanta, and Dallas who hoped to live out the Biblical
story.

Some travelers had arrived at Ghana's Accra Airport,
expecting customs agents to embrace them, porters to
shout—"welcome," and the taxi drivers to ferry them,
horns blaring, to the city square where smiling officials
would cover them in ribbons and clasp them to their
breasts with tearful sincerity. Our arrival had little impact
on anyone but us. We ogled the Ghanaians and few of
them even noticed. The newcomers hid disappointment in
quick repartee, in jokes and clenched jaws.

The citizens were engaged in their own concerns. They
were busy adoring their flag, their five-year-old independence from Britain and their president. Journalists, using
a beautiful language created by wedding English words to
an African syntax, described their leader as "Kwame
Nkrumah, man who surpasses man, iron which cuts iron."
Orators, sounding more like Baptist southern preachers
than they knew, spoke of Ghana, the jewel of Africa lead-

ing the entire continent from colonialism to full independence by the grace of Nkrumah and God, in that order. When Nkrumah ordered the nation to detribalize, the Fanti, Twi, Ashanti, Ga and Ewe clans began busily dismantling formations which had been constructed centuries earlier by their forefathers. Having the responsibility of building a modern country, while worshipping traditional ways and gods, consumed enormous energies.

As the Ghanaians operated an efficient civil service, hotels, huge dams, they were still obliged to be present at customary tribal rituals. City streets and country roads were hosts daily to files of celebrants of mourners, accompanied by drums, en route to funerals, outdoorings (naming ceremonies), marriages or the installations of chiefs, and they celebrated national and religious harvest days. It is small wonder that the entrance of a few Black Americans into that high stepping promenade went largely unnoticed.

The wonder, however, was neither small nor painless to the immigrants. We had come to Africa from our varying starting places and with myriad motives, gaping with hungers, some more ravenous than others, and we had little tolerance for understanding being ignored. At least we wanted someone to embrace us and maybe congratulate us because we had survived. If they felt the urge, they could thank us for having returned.

We, who had been known for laughter, continued to smile. There was a gratifying irony in knowing that the first family of Black Americans in Ghana were the Robert Lees of Virginia, where the first Africans, brought in bondage to the American Colonies in 1619, were deposited. Robert and Sarah Lee were Black dentists who had studied at Lincoln University in Pennsylvania with the young Kwame Nkrumah, and had come in 1957 to Ghana to celebrate its just won independence. They returned a year later with their two sons to become Ghanaian citizens.

The Lees and the presence of W.E.B. Du Bois and Alphaeus Hunton nearly legitimized all of us.

Dr. Du Bois and his wife Shirley Graham had been personally invited by the President to spend the rest of their lives in Ghana. Dr. Hunton had come from the United States with his wife Dorothy to work with Dr. Du Bois on the ambitious Encyclopedia Africana.

The rest of the Black Americans, who buzzed mothlike on the periphery of acceptance, were separated into four distinct groups.

There were over forty families, some with children, who had come simply and as simply moved into the countryside hoping to melt onto the old landscape. They were teachers and farmers.

The second group had come under the aegis of the American government and were viewed with suspicion by Ghanaians, and Black Americans stayed apart from them as well. Too often they mimicked the manners of their former lords and ladies, trying to treat the Africans as Whites had treated them. They socialized with Europeans and White Americans, fawning upon that company with ugly obsequiousness.

There was a minuscule business community which had found a slight but unsure footing in Accra.

Julian's circle had stupendous ambitions and thought of itself as a cadre of political émigrés. Its members were impassioned and volatile, dedicated to Africa, and Africans at home and abroad. We, for I counted myself in that company, felt that we would be the first accepted and once taken in and truly adopted, we would hold the doors open until all Black Americans could step over our feet, enter through the hallowed portals and come home at last.

Guy, wearing a metal and leather neck brace, enrolled in the university and moved happily into Mensah Sarbah Dormitory Hall. I was surprised and delighted to find that being alone brought a deeply satisfying bliss. I hummed, sang to myself, strutted, cooked and entertained for a month before the professor returned and claimed his house.

The YWCA wasn't as sterile on my second stay. I had a job, a car, some money and amusing friends.

All meals were served in the ground floor dining room under the watchful eyes of Directress Vivian Baeta, the daughter of a Ghanaian clergyman. Miss Baeta was young and pleasant, but a little too correct for our tastes. She frowned upon loud voices and noisy laughter and most diners, often white collar workers from nearby office buildings who filled the restaurant each mealtime, acceded to her wishes. The Black American residents, however, having no living room save Julian's side porch, used the dining room as a place to gather, to talk, to argue and maybe to flirt with male friends before returning to the celibate cells on the second floor.

Although we tried to respect Miss Baeta's desires, passion dictated the volume of our conversations. The directress's disapproving look fell upon us frequently.

One lunch time Vicki, Alice and I were occupying our usual table when a voice louder than any tone we had ever used split the quiet air.

"No rye?" Again, "No rye? What fa country you peepo got? No rye?" A huge, six-foot-tall woman was standing at a window table. She wore West African cloth, her head tie was large and beautifully wrapped, and she was angry.

"You peepo! You Ghanaians. You got yourself your Kwame Nkrumah, but you got no rye. Last night, you give the peepo cassava. Breakfast you give us garri. Lunch you give us yam. Still no rye." She was complaining specifically to the persons in charge who were nowhere to be seen. Miss Baeta had poked her head into the dining room, seen the irate woman, and had hastily withdrawn. Other diners put their heads dangerously close to their plates as if searching for some microscopic intruder in their food.

The woman continued. "I come to you peepose country from Sierra Leone where we serve rye. I know this country is proud Ghana, but it still is Africa and you don't give me rye. You think you England? You think you German? Where is the rye?"

The woman was demanding rice and I quickly sympathized with her. The grandmother who raised me was a firm believer in rice. The only white newspapers which reached our house were brought at grandmother's request by maids oncoming from work. Momma was a good cook who experimented with the exotic recipes she found in the White papers. She would prepare Italian spaghetti, macaroni and cheese, scalloped potatoes, O'Brien potatoes, creamed noodles, but still she served rice with each meal. The family was not obliged to eat the rice if we were pleased with the other starches, but Momma never felt the table was properly set until the filled rice bowl was placed in its usual spot.

The African woman was screaming, "You peepo, you got your Black Star Square. You got your university, but you got no rye! You peepo!" She began to laugh sarcastically, "You make me laugh. Pitiful peepo. Pitiful. No rye, no pride. Ha, ha. See me, Sierra Leone woman, laugh. Ha, ha. Ha, ha!"

I went through the private doors into the kitchen. The cook was sitting on a stool drinking a soda. I said, "Uncle, please excuse me." He looked up frowning, apparently expecting one more complaint.

"Uncle, there is a woman out there who is dying for rice."

He shook his head. "Rice tonight. For dinner. Rice tonight."

I said in a sweet voice, "Oh please, Uncle. She must have rice. Please."

He said, "She must wait, or go somewhere else. Rice tonight."

I was defeated. I turned to leave, then turned back. "The woman will go back to her home thinking Ghanaians are mean."

"Let her go. Rice tonight! Anyway, where is she from?" He wasn't really interested. I had my hand on the door. I said, "Sierra Leone."

The cook jumped off the stool. "Why didn't you say that? You said 'a woman.' I thought you meant a Black American. Sierra Leone people can't live without rice. They are like people from Liberia. They die for rice. I will bring her some."

The woman was still standing and talking to the air, although weakly, when the cook passed through the dining room bearing a large platter of rice. He placed it on the woman's table without a word, and she sat down speechless, her eyes hungrily counting the white grains.

When the cook reached the kitchen door the room exploded in applause.

The University of Ghana with its white buildings and red tiled roofs loomed like a chimera atop Legon's green hills. The Moroccan architecture of arches, wide, low steps and loggia gave the institution an unusually inviting warmth. African students and faculty paraded the halls and grounds in distinctive and often colorful outfits.

Women often wore short cotton skirts and blouses or the richly patterned long national dress, consisting of provocatively cut peplum blouses and long, tight skirts meant to accent small waists and abundant hips.

Some men wore the northern territory woven smocks which were highlighted with bright embroidery, while some others favored Western slacks and short sleeved shirts. Moslems from Nigeria or Cameroon wore the Grand Bou Bou: twelve yards of fine cotton fashioned into pants, shirts and a matching floor length over-smock. Despite the hot weather there were a few African professors who elected to wear the Cambridge or Oxford school gowns over woolen pants, buttoned down shirts and ties. Some wore Nehru jackets made popular by President Nkrumah. It was not surprising to see a lecturer in national dress on Monday, a casual smock and slacks on Tuesday, and worsted tweed on Wednesday. Ghana's colorful cloth was sold in every marketplace, so status could not be determined by clothes. Thus the market woman, the bank teller and the student might wear the same pattern on any morning and nothing was thought of the coincidence. A fragrance of flowers permeated that riot of color, sound and activity provoking all the senses into constant exercise.

My office door opened onto a grassy courtyard and the windows looked out onto a dance pavilion. Students, faculty, tradesmen, market women selling roasted peanuts and plaintain, visitors and administrators were in constant view. Astonishingly, in that strain of energy projects were designed and work was completed.

Efua wrote and directed plays. The handsome Joe de Graft taught acting, and occasionally graced the stage with a quite heroic presence. Bertie Okpoku and Grace Nuamah taught the traditional dances of the Ashanti, Ewe, and Ga people. Professor Nketia, with disarming gentleness, controlled all the artistic temperaments while teaching music, music theory, music history, and African musicology.

I worked wherever I was needed. Professor wrote *Kple, Music of the Gods,* a book on the liturgy of the Ewe, and despite my scanty knowledge of typewriters, I was asked to type the manuscript, and did so. Reports on students' development, their absences and illnesses were kept in my files. Sometimes I handled theatre reservations or sold tickets at the box office in town. When Ireland's Abbey

Theatre director, Bryd Lynch, came to teach at Legon, she chose to present Bertolt Brecht's *Mother Courage* in full production, and I was chosen to play the title role.

My son was growing into manhood on the university campus, under my eye, but not my thumb. Ana Livia and Julian, Efua and her children, my housemates and our lusty friends provided recreation enough. At last life was getting itself in joint.

Vicki, Alice and I had decided to share a house, and the pretty white bungalow we found was a proud prize. There were three bedrooms (Vicki characteristically offered to take the smallest), a commodious living room and dining room. The kitchen was a disappointment to me, but my housemates, who claimed no interest in cooking, hardly noticed its meagre appointments.

Vicki Garvin was a pretty little yellow woman, always immaculately groomed with tiny, graceful hands. She had been a national union organizer in the United States and was highly respected in American and European labor circles, and had come to Africa in the legion of hopeful returnees. She was strong-nerved, but years of unsuccessful bargaining with American bosses and reluctant workers had left cynicism in her voice and her face was quick to adopt a shadow. She had a Bachelor's degree in English, a Master's degree in economics and years of experience.

She had gone first to Nigeria, but after a bitter reception, or rather, a bitter rejection, had been encouraged to believe that she would easily find creative work in the progressive country of Ghana.

For months she carried her qualifications as burnt offerings to labor and trade union offices, and when not ignored outright she was told "the big man," meaning the boss, "is travelling. Come again." When Vicki did find work it was as a typist in a foreign embassy. She refused rancor, saying that right now "Ghana needs its jobs for Ghanaians, but someday. . . ."

Alice Windom, the youngest in the bungalow, was also the most explosive. She was a dark mahogany color, had a wide open smile and the prettiest legs in Accra. Men used to sit in our living room, oblivious to the exquisite conversation of three bright women, too busy ogling and loving Alice's legs. Alice had degrees from an Ohio university and a Master's from the prestigious University of Chicago. Her argumentative talents, so recently exercised in the school environments, were as pointed as broken bones.

She had come from a family of university professors, and had debated with her siblings for dominance. Neither visitors nor the other bungalow inhabitants could best her in verbal contests. During her last school years, she had vowed to save her money and come to Ghana to live forever. Her field was sociology and her dream was to belong to a community of African social workers. She searched in associations and congresses and committees, but her diligence went unrewarded. Alice became a receptionist in a foreign embassy.

As was expected, Alice was not as casual as Vicki on being denied a chance to work in her field of interest. "Damn, these Africans in personnel are treating me like Charlie did down on the plantation." There was never a suggestion that she might leave Ghana for greener pastures.

It was agreed in the house that as far as work was concerned, I was the most fortunate. As administrative assistant at the University of Ghana, I had direct contact with African students, faculty, administrators and small traders. While the job was a blessing, the pay was not bounteous.

I received no housing, tuition, or dislocation allowances. On the first day of every month, when the small manilla envelopes of cash were delivered to the offices, I would open mine with a confusion of sensations. Seventy-five pounds. Around two hundred dollars. In San Francisco, my mother spent that amount on two pairs of shoes. Then I would think, seventy-five pounds, what luck! Many Ghanaians at the university would take home half that much with gratitude. My feelings slid like mercury. Seventy-five pounds. Sheer discrimination. The old British philosopher's packet was crammed with four times that, and all I ever saw him do was sit in the Lecturers' Lounge ordering Guinness stout and dribbling on about Locke and Lord Acton and the British Commonwealth.

I would count out the paper money, loving the Black president's picture. Thirty pounds for rent; thirty for my son's tuition, being paid on the installment plan; ten for beer, cigarettes, food. Another five for the houseman who my friends and I paid fifteen pounds per month to clean the bungalow.

A grown man could live on fifteen pounds, and there I

was being a simpering ass. I was my mother's daughter. When I left her house at seventeen, she had said, "I'm not worried about you. You'll do your best, and you might succeed. And remember, as long as you're making a living for yourself you can take care of your baby. It's no trouble to pack double." All I had to do was find extra work.

The editor's office of the *Ghanaian Times* had all the excitement of a busy city intersection. People came, left, talked, shouted, laid down papers, picked up packages, spoke English, Fanti, Twi, Ga and Pidgin on the telephone or to each other.

T. D. Kwesi Bafoo perched behind his desk as if it was the starting mark for a one hundred yard sprint. At a signal he would leap up and hurl himself past me, through the crowded room and out of the door.

His cheeks, brows, eyes and hands moved even before he talked.

I said, "I am a journalist. I've brought some examples of my work. These are from the *Arab Observer* in Cairo." He waved away my folder and said, "We know who you are. A good writer, and that you are a Nkrumaist." I was certainly the latter and not yet the former.

As he stuffed papers into a briefcase he asked, "Can you write a piece on America today?"

"Today? Do you mean right now?"

He looked at me and grinned, "No. America today. America, capitalism and racial prejudice."

"In one article?" I didn't want him to know the request was implausible.

He said, "A sort of overview. You understand?"

I asked, seriously, "How many words, three thousand?"

He answered without looking at me, "Three hundred. Just the high points."

The seething energy would no longer be contained. Bafoo was on his feet and around the desk before I could rise.

"We'll pay you the standard fee. Have it here by Friday. I have another meeting. Pleasure meeting you. Good-bye."

He passed and disappeared through the door before I had gathered my purse and briefcase. I imagined him running up to the next appointment, arriving there in a heat, simmering during the meeting, then racing away to the next, and on and on. The picture of Mr. Bafoo so entertained me that I was outside on the street before the realization came to me that I had another job which paid "the standard fee." I was earning that at the university. In order to afford luxuries I had to look further.

The Ghana Broadcasting office was as to the *Times* newspaper office what a drawing room was to a dance hall. The lobby was large, well furnished and quiet. A receptionist, pretty and dressed in western clothes, looked at me so quizzically, I thought perhaps she knew something I needed to know.

She frowned, wrinkling her careful loveliness. "Yes? You want to talk to someone about writing?" Her voice was as crisp as a freshly starched and ironed doily.

I said, "Yes. I am a writer."

She shook her head, "But who? Who do you want to talk to?" She couldn't believe in my ignorance.

I said, "I don't know. I suppose the person who hires writers."

"But what is his name?" She had begun to smile, and I heard her sarcasm.

"I don't know his name. Don't you know it?" I knew that hostility would gain me nothing but the front door, so I tried to charm her. "I mean, surely you know who I should see." I gave her a little submissive smile and knew that if I got a job I'd never speak to her again.

She dismissed my attempt at flattery by saying curtly, "I am the receptionist. It is my job to know everyone in the building," and picked up the morning paper.

I persisted, "Well, who should I see?"

She looked up from the page and smiled patronizingly. "You should see who you want to see. Who do you want to see?" She knew herself to be a cat and I was a wounded bird. I decided to remove myself from her grasp. I leaned forward and imitating her accent. I said, "You silly ass, you can take a flying leap and go straight to hell."

Her smile never changed. "American Negroes are always crude."

I stood nailed to the floor. Her knowledge of my people could only have been garnered from hearsay, and the few old American movies which tacked on Black characters as awkwardly as the blinded attach paper tails to donkey caricatures.

We were variably excited, exciting, jovial, organic, paranoid, hearty, lusty, loud, raucous, grave, sad, forlorn, silly and forceful. We had all the rights and wrongs human flesh and spirit are heir to. On behalf of my people, I should have spoken. I needed to open my mouth and give lie to her statement, but as usual my thoughts were too many and muddled to be formed into sentences. I turned and left the office.

The incident brought me close to another facet of Ghana, Africa, and of my own mania.

The woman's cruelty activated a response which I had developed under the exacting tutelage of masters. Her brown skin, curly hair, full lips, wide flanged nostrils notwithstanding, I had responded to her as if she was a rude White salesclerk in an American department store.

Was it possible that I and all American Blacks had been wrong on other occasions? Could the cutting treatment we often experienced have been stimulated by something other than our features, our hair and color? Was the odor of old slavery so obvious that people were offended and lashed out at us automatically? Had what we judged as racial prejudice less to do with race and more to do with our particular ancestors' bad luck at having been caught, sold and driven like beasts?

The receptionist and I could have been sisters, or in fact, might be cousins far removed. Yet her scorn was no different from the supercilious rejections of Whites in the United States. In Harlem and in Tulsa, in San Francisco and in Atlanta, in all the hamlets and cities of America, Black people maimed, brutalized, abused and murdered each other daily and particularly on bloody Saturday nights. Were we only and vainly trying to kill that portion of our history which we could neither accept nor deny? The questions temporarily sobered my intoxication with Africa. For a few days, I examined whether in looking for a home I, and all the émigrés, were running from a bitter truth that rode lightly but forever at home on our shoulders.

The company of my companions, Guy's returning robust health, and Efua's friendship weened me away from my unease and the questions. I would not admit that if I couldn't be comfortable in Africa, I had no place else to go.

I turned my back to the niggling insecurities and opened my arms again to Ghana.

I wanted my hair fixed Ghanaian fashion and didn't want to spend time in a hot beauty shop. I made an appointment for a home visitor.

The laughing Comfort Adday was a stenographer as well as a beautician. She told me "Sistah, I don't work. My fingers work. Work is for farmers. As for my part, I try hard to stay away from farms." She pulled patches of my hair and wound them with coarse black thread. "I have to save myself for later. For children. Then when I get ready, for a husband."

Peals rang over my head as she seemed to wrench my hair out of its roots. "You only have the one boy, eh?" I tried to nod, but my head was in a vise. I mumbled, "Yes." She said, "But my deah," laughter . . . "You know they say 'one child is no child.' "

I had heard the saying but couldn't nod and chose not

to mumble again. Comfort continued, making her voice low and suggestive, "And they say, too, 'if you don't use it you'll lose it.'" Here her laughter rose and her hands pulled, jerking me nearly to a standing position. "You're not a chicken, you know, Sistah." I was over thirty. "Not to say you are too old to lay eggs." She tugged a scrap of hair and luckily left my head attached to my neck. "But you keep waiting, your egg maker will grow grey." Her laughter exceeded all earlier efforts, "and any chicks that come," tug, wrestle, jerk, "will walk out fully dressed, playing the drums." Jubilation at her own wit and wisdom bent her body in half, but her fingers never ceased pulling my hair or coiling the black thread against my scalp.

"Sistah, look at yourself." She released me. Her face, the color of ancient bricks, was groomed with a proud smile. I went to the mirror. Long, black spikes jutted from my head in every direction, and long strings hung to my shoulders. It was a fashion worn by the pickaninnies whose photographs I had seen and hated in old books. I was aghast. No wonder she had laughed so heartily. I quickly searched her face for ridicule, but respect for her work was all I found.

I stuttered. "But, I wanted, ... I didn't want ..." I could neither go in the street with that hairdo, nor was I capable of unwinding the cord that now shone on my hair with an evil gleam. For some unknown reason the beautician had chosen to teach me a lesson on the foolishness of trying to "go native."

"Sistah, now sit down, let me finish."

"I thought you were finished." My voice came weakly and was drowned out by her great laughter. "Oh sistah, oh my deah." She had to hold her stomach which threatened to shake itself loose from her body. "Oh Sistah. I just told you that I knew you weren't a spring chick. If I let you go out like that, they'd catch both of us and put us in the silly folks hospital."

The agony of laughter left her face slowly. "No sistah, my deah, only young girls whose time has not come can wear their hair like that."

She gathered the dangling strings and pulled them tightly together. Her fingers moved quickly over my head. After a few minutes she picked up scissors from a stool and with a few snips, removed the last hanging strings.

"Now look. See yourself, and tell me."

I looked in the mirror and was relieved that I looked like every other Ghanaian woman. My hair was pulled tightly into small neat patches and the triangular designs of tan scalp and black hair was as exact as the design in tweed cloth.

"Sistah, you have given me such a good laugh, I shouldn't charge you." Comfort was washing her combs and rolling her scissors and thread in a cotton white cloth. I knew that last statement was only for show.

In just six months I learned that Ghanaian women might take in orphans, give generously to the poor, and feed every person who came to their houses. They could allow their men certain sexual freedom, but they were very strict in money matters. When it came to finances "Ghana women no play, oh," had been said to or around me hundreds of times.

I paid Comfort.

She said, "I will come again in two weeks. Oh, how I like to laugh with you."

I didn't want to wonder whether she was sincere, but I noticed that I hadn't laughed even once.

A Black couple who had just arrived in Africa sat in our living room explaining their presence on the Continent.

"Because of Nkrumah" (The man pronounced the President's name NeeKrumah) "and Sékou Touré, we decided it was either Ghana or Guinea. We have come to Mother Africa to suckle from her breasts." The man spoke so vigorously his Afro trembled and his long neck carried his head from side to side. He wore a brightly colored African shirt and reminded me of a large exotic bird.

Alice spoke angrily, "Hell man, you ought to be ashamed of yourself. Talking about sucking from Africa's breasts. When you were born Black in America, you were born weaned."

I said, "Africa doesn't need anybody as big as you pulling on her tits."

Vicki said, "And that's an ugly metaphor."

The man was sparring quickly. "The Zulus use it."

"But you're a Black American," I reminded him.

"Yeah. Well, who is to say my ancestors weren't Zulus?"

In just a few months our living room had begun to compete with the Mayfield side porch for popularity. Late nights found us drinking beer and fastidious over even the smallest points in a conversation.

Alice earned her reputation as the most formidable disputant. Having spent her working hours answering telephone calls and receiving embassy visitors, she looked eagerly toward the evenings and weekends. Then she could exercise her sharp mind and quick tongue on anyone within hearing range.

The wise Vicki said, "What Africa needs is help. After centuries of slavers taking her strongest sons and daughters, after years of colonialism, Africa needs her progeny to bring something to her."

Alice grinned, warming up. She said, "I've never seen Africa as a woman, and somewhere I resent the use of any sexual pronoun to describe this complex continent. It's not he or she. It is more an it."

The visitors looked disapprovingly at us all. The need to believe in Africa's maternal welcome was painfully obvious. They didn't want to know that they had not come home, but had left one familiar place of painful memory for another strange place with none.

The woman, whose large natural matched her husband's, sat like a broken doll. Her brown face was still, her dark eyes flat and staring. I would not have been too surprised had she cried, "Maa Maa, Maa Maa" in a tiny toy voice.

Alice said, "The Sahara continues to eat up arable land at a frightening rate, and nomadic people continue to herd cattle which eat every blade of grass that pops up. What the continent needs is about five hundred artesian well diggers and about five hundred agronomists. That would have been a gift to bring."

"I belong here. My ancestors were taken from this land." The visitor was fighting back.

"Of course, you're right." Vicki's voice was soothing.

"And under ideal conditions you could return and even lay claim to an ancestral inheritance. But Alice has a good point. The continent is poor, and while Ghanaians have wonderful spirits, thanks to themselves and Kwame Nkrumah, they are desperate."

I asked, "What did you do at home? What is your work?"

The man was still silent, and I had spoken only to put sound into the sad silence.

Vicki offered advice, "Ghana would be easier than Guinea, unless you speak French."

The woman's voice was a surprisingly rich contralto. "He worked in the Chicago stockyards, and I was a Bunny."

She got our total and immediate attention. Although she wore no makeup and a sleeved dress of a demure cut, it was easy to imagine her in a bunny costume. She muttered just above a whisper, "We've been saving for two years."

Her husband stood up scowling, "Don't tell them anything, Hon. It's just like Negroes. They are here, in their own place, and they don't want us in. Just like crabs in a bucket. Pulling the other one down. When will you people learn? Let's go."

They would have been surprised to learn that we were no less annoyed with them than they with us. They were just two more people in an unceasing parade of naïve travelers who thought that an airline ticket to Africa would erase the past and open wide the gates to a perfect future. Possibly we saw our now seldom expressed hopes in the ingenuous faces of the new arrivals.

Vicki waved her small hands. "Wait a minute. You don't understand."

"Come on, Hon. The taxi driver was wrong."

I asked, "What taxi driver?"

The woman answered, "We don't know his name. He was driving us around and when he found out we were Americans, he said he was going to take us to a Black American home. That's how we got here."

We looked at each other knowing the danger of getting a reputation of inhospitality in this country, where we were striving for welcome.

Alice lit a fresh cigarette from an old one. "I guess because we talk so much, folks have the idea that we know something, so Black Americans come here or to Julian Mayfield's house. We weren't trying to discourage you from staying in Ghana. We just wanted to prepare you for what you might, no, what you will encounter so you won't be disappointed."

Vicki added, "Sort of immunizing you before you get the disease."

I added, "We're trying to explain that if you expect Africans to open their arms and homes to you, you'll be in for a terrible shock. Not that they will be unkind. Never unkind, but most of them will be distant. One problem, of course, is our inability to speak the language. Without a language it is very difficult to communicate." The man's anger had propelled him to the door. I touched his sleeve and said, "Don't rush off. Have dinner with us."

All people use food for more reasons than mere nutrition, and I was hoping that in the present case it would work to calm our visitors' ruffled feathers.

The husband acted as if he still wanted to leave, but was persuaded by his wife to stay.

As I had hoped, they relaxed during dinner and allowed themselves to be charmed by Alice, who worked at being her clever best. She made them laugh at her Chicago stories, Vicki related tales of Paul Robeson, and I talked about my years in show business.

We stood at the door saying good-bye when the man, all seriousness again, shook Alice's hand. "I think we'll go to Guinea. If we have to learn a foreign language to be accepted in Africa, we may as well learn French."

The woman waved. "We certainly appreciate the dinner and your advice. Hope we meet again."

That they had missed our clearly made points boded well for them. They just might succeed in their search for the illusive Africa, which secreted itself when approached directly, like a rain forest on a moonless night. Africa might just deliver itself into their hands because they matched its obliqueness.

The telephone call brought unsettling news. The secretary's voice simply said, "You are wanted at the *Ghanaian Times.*" I sped to the office building, accompanied by nervous excitement. Had my article been accepted, or had the editor discovered what I already knew; that in order to write about the United States, capitalism and racial prejudice one needed a lifetime, three hundred thousand words, and a lot of luck?

T. D. Bafoo was on his feet when I arrived at his desk.

"Maya!" He waved my pages at me and as usual spoke in short explosions. "This is good, Sister! You Black Americans know a thing or two, don't you?" He spoke too quickly for me to respond.

"We will have a new baby, you know?" I didn't.

"And we will invite you to the outdooring, in the country."

An outdooring is the first African rite of passage. It always begins at dawn, eight days after the child's birth, and gives family and friends a chance to see and welcome the newest soul.

"I am asking Alice, Vicki, and Julian and others! Come! Black Americans must see how we salute life! Party! We have a great party for life!"

"Come to my house, here tonight in Accra. Greet my wife. I will tell you how to come to us in Kanda."

I thanked him, took his address, smiled and was again left standing as he hurried away.

The modesty of T. D.'s pretty bungalow was surprising. He was a Big Man, and even in Nkrumah's best of all worlds, Big Men often lived in coarse ostentation. Some owned huge castle-like houses and were driven by chauffeurs through the streets of Ghana in Mercedes-Benzes and limousines. Although most cabinet ministers, members of Parliament, government administrators, and wealthy businessmen wore the common matching shirt and pants which had been popularized by the President, their wealth and power were not held in secret. Wives, mistresses, girlfriends, and female relatives were known to wear heavy gold necklaces and bracelets to market and to import expensive furniture from Europe. It was not unknown for some Big Men and their women to treat the servant class as slaves. They were generally unpopular, and in safe company they were ridiculed, but their power was threatening and little was said of them in public.

A smiling T. D. met me at the door. "Sister, come, come inside. You are finally here. You are at home, and meet my wife. Come, we will eat foo foo and garden eggs." Although he still spoke as if he needed to cram everything into one sentence, he was a quieter man in his own house.

His wife was a tall, brown woman with an earnest face and a beautiful voice, and was very pregnant. She smiled and took my hand.

"Sister Maya. *Akwaba.* Welcome. I am making chicken for you, since you can't eat fish."

T. D. grinned, "Sister, news travels in Ghana. We know everything or nothing. Come, we will have beer. What do you like?"

Beer preferences were fiercely defended or opposed. The two vying brands were Star and Club.

"I'm a Club person myself." I spoke as proudly as I had heard Ghanaians do.

"Ye! Ye! I knew you were okay. I am Club too. All Star drinkers are untrustworthy. Differences between good and bad beer drinkers are stronger than the imperialist introduced divisions between Africans. Don't you think so, Sister?" T. D. laughed like a boy and took me into his study. "We will drink in here." He spoke to his wife, "Join us when you can."

We sat down in a room crowded with books and papers and magazines. Mrs. Bafoo spoke from the doorway, "Kwesi, are you going to give Sister Maya your famous speech? You would do better if you stand on the chair." She entered carrying beer and laughing.

T. D. had the grace to drop his head. When he looked at me his eyes were sharp with mischief. "Sister, I am Fanti. This woman is a nurse, but she is also an Ewe. A terrible mixture. Nurses think they know the body and Ewes think they know the mind. Oh boy, what have I married?"

I spent the afternoon eating with my fingers and listening to T. D.'s political discussions. I experimented with my Fanti, much to the amusement of my hosts, and found that while I had a reasonable vocabulary, my melody was not in tune. T. D. suggested I pick up Ewe, but when I heard Mrs. Bafoo sing-speak her language, I decided I would continue struggling to master Fanti.

The couple, throughout the evening, tenderly but relentlessly teased each other about their mixed marriage, laughing at their differences, each gibe a love pat, sweetly intimate.

I left after nightfall with directions to T. D.'s country place, and the feeling that maybe the new friendship would lead me behind the modern face of Ghana and I could get a glimpse of Africa's ancient tribal soul. That soul was a skittish thing. Each time I had approached it, bearing a basket of questions that plagued me, it withdrew, closed down, disguising itself into sensual pleasantries. It had many distracting guiles.

The musical names of Ghana's cities were lovely on the tongue and caressing to the ears; Kumasi (Koo mah see), Koforidua (Ko fo rid you ah), Mpraeso (Um prah eh so). Ghanaians boasted that Accra and Sekondi were old towns showing proof of trade with Europeans in the fifteenth century. I loved to imagine a long-dead relative trading in those marketplaces, fishing from that active sea and living in those exotic towns, but the old anguish would not let me remain beguiled.

Unbidden would come the painful reminder—"Not all slaves were stolen, nor were all slave dealers European." Suppose my great-grandfather was enslaved in that colorful town by his brother. Imagine my great-grandmother traded by her sister in that marketplace.

Were those laughing people who moved in the streets with such equanimity today descendants of slave-trading families? Did that one's ancestor sell mine or did that grandmother's grandmother grow fat on the sale of my grandmother's grandmother?

At first when those baleful thoughts interrupted my pleasant reveries I chased them away, only to learn that they had the resistance of new virus and the vitality to pop into my thoughts, unasked, at odd and often awkward times.

So I had been intrigued watching T. D. and his wife using their tribal differences to demonstrate their love. Getting to know them might lay to rest the ugly suspicion that my ancestors had been weak and gullible and were sold into bondage by a stronger and more clever tribe. The idea was hideous, and if true, I was forced to conclude that my own foreparents probably abstained from the brutish sale of others simply because they couldn't find tribes more gullible and vulnerable than they. I couldn't decide what would be the most appalling; to be descended from bullies or to be a descendant of dupes.

The Bafoos' love could erase the idea that African slavery stemmed mostly from tribal exploitation.

On a midmorning break I went into the Senior Common Room. My entry made no impact on the confident people who continued their conversation, offering their voices to each other as beautiful women offer their hands to homely suitors.

The Englishman was speaking desultorily through a thin nose, "I understand their anger. I do think it is unattractive, but I understand it."

A Yugoslav woman, too intellectual for cosmetics, argued without passion, "But they have been treated like beasts."

The Englishman was a little petulant, "That doesn't give them the right to act bestial."

A Canadian attempted to bring balance. "While it isn't a laudable response, it is understandable. The effects of cruel treatment die slowly."

The Englishman said, "Look here, they've been there three hundred years, why the devil are they starting up now?" He raised his voice and ordered, "Another beer, Kojo. Fact, beer all around."

He was an irritated Ronald Colman in an old movie. I sat in a corner drinking tepid beer, knowing I had walked in on a theatrical set and that I would be wise to either sit quietly or exit stage left.

The Ghanaian steward, old and doddering, understood "all around" did not include me, so he took bottles to the large table and went back to his stool behind the counter.

The Senior Common Room at the Institute of African Studies was reserved for professors, lecturers and some administrators. Although it was filled with ancient furniture and a persevering odor of beer, some employees from other faculties at Legon University preferred it to their own lounges. I supposed its popularity could be credited to the nearby Faculty of Music and Dance. At any moment in the day pretty girls and half-dressed men rushed past its door en route to dance classes. Master drummers gave demonstrations hourly outdoors behind the building. Singers practicing in the high-pitched Ghanaian tones could be heard in the area stereophonically. The lounge itself was stuffy, but the surrounding area was fresh and appealing.

The German professor from another department spoke loudly, "Old Man," he said, attempting a British accent, "it's understandable that you're tired of unrest. Your empires have exhausted you."

The Englishman answered, "I don't know about my empire," he pronounced it "empiah," "but agitation becomes a bore after a while."

The Yugoslav woman was ready for a fight. "But not to the agitators."

The Canadian spoke and the room was no longer a set, nor were the people characters I could laugh at or ignore. He said calmly, "But American Negroes are not the masses. They are only about ten percent of the U.S. population."

They were talking about Black Americans. I was sure that the recent riot in Harlem which had been front-page news in Ghana had stimulated the discussion. I focused to listen and to find a place to enter.

"More beer, Kojo, please." The Yugoslav woman's voice was as neat as her body and clothes were abandoned. "I put it to you that the American Negroes are fed up with the system because Democracy does not work. They feel that they are proof."

The old long-snout Briton popped up, "Democracy was never created for the lower classes. Everyone knows that. Just like at Ghana."

As I was gathering a response to singe their ears, a Ghanaian professor of English walked in. He went to the crowded table and said, "Hello, old chums." Without turning to face the steward, he raised his voice. "Beer all around, Kojo." He pulled out a chair and sat. "You were saying 'just look at Ghana.' What about my country?"

I let my preparation scatter. Here was the proper person who would have the arch counterstatement.

The Englishman was already bored with the conversation, but he forced himself to respond. He said, "Democracy which has never worked anyway, was never intended for the masses. And I gave Ghana as evidence."

The African accepted his beer, and without a glance at the steward, poured a glass and drank.

"Hum," he licked his lips. "Delicious. We may not make a great democracy, but no one can complain that we don't make a good beer. What?"

The Europeans laughed and the African joined in. They had assassinated my people as well as my new country. I looked at the steward, but his face was passive and his eyes focused on the open door.

I raised my voice and said, "Obviously you people think you've got all the answers. Well, you should wait until someone who really cares asks you a question. You don't know a damn thing about Black Americans, and I resent every stupid thing you've said."

It wasn't going well at all. My brain was not responding properly. I needed to be sharp, cutting, and politely rude in order to reach their hardened ears, and all I had done was blubber.

I said, "You people are idiots, and you dare speak of Ghana. You rejects." I was surprised to find myself standing and my voice loud and screeching. "You left your old cold ass countries and came here where you've never had it so good. Now you've got servants and can bathe more than once a month. It's a pity more of you don't take advantage of the opportunity. You stinking bastards."

Rage piloted me to the door. "And don't say a word to me, I'll slap the water out of all of you."

I always knew that fury was my natural enemy. It clotted my blood and clogged my pores. It literally blinded me so that I lost peripheral vision. My mouth tasted of metal, and I couldn't breathe through my nostrils. My thighs felt weak and there was a prickling sensation in my armpits and my groin. I longed to drop on the path to my office, but I continued ordering my reluctant body forward.

"Professor?" A soft voice turned me around. The steward was there smiling as if I was a child who had acted mischievously.

He asked, "Professor, why you let them disturb your heart?"

I stuttered, "They were—" I knew the steward was un-educated, but surely he understood the rude scene that had occurred.

"They were insulting my people. I couldn't just sit there."

His smile never changed. "And your people, they my people?"

"Yes, but—I mean American Blacks."

"They been insulted before?"

"Yes—but . . ."

"And they still live?"

"Yes, but . . . they also insulted Ghana, your country."

"Oh Sister, as for that one, it's nothing."

"Nothing?" He was not only uneducated, I thought he was stupid as well.

He said, "This is not their place. In time they will pass. Ghana was here when they came. When they go, Ghana will be here. They are like mice on an elephant's back. They will pass."

In that second I was wounded. My mind struck a truth as an elbow can strike a table edge. A poor, uneducated servant in Africa was so secure he could ignore established White rudeness. No Black American I had ever known knew that security. Our tenure in the United States, though long and very hard-earned, was always so shaky, we had developed patience as a defense, but never as ag-gression.

I needed to know more. I said, "But that African. He is a part of that group."

"No, Sistah. He is a part of Africa. He just a Beentoo."

Beentoo was a derisive word used for a person who had studied abroad and returned to Ghana with European airs. The steward continued, "He's been to the United

Kingdom. Been to the United States. In time, that posing will pass. Now he is at home, and home will take him back."

He reached out his arm and touched my shoulder. "Don't let them trouble your heart. In a way you are a 'Beentoo' too. But your people . . . they from this place, and if this place claims you or if it does not claim you, here you belong."

He turned and shuffled back to the lounge.

The steward, Otu, and I were in the kitchen. Since I prepared all the food, he was second cook. He washed and diced vegetables, cleaned the utensils as I finished using them and generally made my job easy.

"Auntie?" It was a name of respect.

"Uncle," I responded respectfully.

"There is a boy, Kojo, who would like to speak to you."

"What does he want?"

"Oh, Auntie, should I know?"

Otu didn't look at me directly and I knew the conversation promised to be as formal as a Japanese tea ceremony.

"Otu, if you do not know, I shall not know. Then I cannot speak to the boy."

My friendship with Efua, reading Ghanaian short

stories and the Fanti I had learned provided me with some insight into the circuitous conversational form.

"Auntie, if I am to say that which I do not know, I will serve neither you, the boy, nor myself." He stopped talking so abruptly I could almost see the period at the end of his sentence. Obviously, we had to start again.

"Uncle?"

"Auntie?"

"This boy who wants to see me, is a nice boy?"

"Yes, Auntie. His family is good. His father and uncles are from my village."

"Kojo is his name?"

"Yes, Kojo."

"And how can I help Kojo, Uncle?"

"Ah Auntie, it is known that you are good." I had found the right key. "This boy would like to work for you, Auntie."

For me? There was nothing I needed done, and if there was I had no money to pay anyone to do it.

"Otu, there is no job here. Please tell him."

"Auntie, he has not asked me for a job. He has asked to speak to you."

Oh, the tortuous subtlety of language. "There is no point . . ." Otu turned, and standing stock-still, looked at me.

I was beaten. I said, "Well, tell him to come around, I will speak to him."

"Yes, Auntie." Otu seldom smiled, but a quick change on his face told me of his pleasure.

"I will get him."

"No, Otu, let's finish dinner. Maybe tomorrow."

"He is just there, Auntie." I followed his nodding head and saw a small figure pressed against the screen door.

"Kojo." Otu's voice was strong with authority. "Kojo, bra."

The door opened and a boy of about fourteen stepped timidly into the room. His smile was both deferring and mischievous. He had heard the entire conversation and knew how I had been maneuvered by Otu.

"Kojo, this is Auntie Maya."

Respectfully, he dropped his eyes, but not before I saw the glint of amusement.

He whispered, "Evening, Auntie."

"Kojo, I'm sorry, but I have no job for you."

"Oh." His head was still bowed.

"Ka. Ka. Ka." Otu spat out the Fanti word meaning speak.

Kojo lifted his eyes and I noticed his resemblance to my beloved brother. He shared with Bailey a rich, dark brown color, small hands and a perfectly round head.

He said, "Auntie, I can do anything. I can shop, and save you money at Makola Market, and even in Bokum Square." Those were the two largest markets in Accra, where the intimidating market women haggled customers to desperation, and they did present a challenge to me.

The boy continued, "I hear Ga and Hausa. I can clean, and I am learning to tailor."

The timidity had been a disguise, he was as lively as young yeast.

"But I shop and I have a dressmaker."

Otu was quietly putting pans away.

"Auntie, I can be your 'small boy.' I can bring you beer and wash your car, and if Wofa Otu will teach me, I can laundry. Auntie, I don't want money. No salary. Just dash."

In West Africa, while tips were not compulsory, they were expected and were called dash.

"Otu?"

"Auntie?"

"Can you use a small boy?"

The older man answered as if I had asked a silly question. "Auntie, all children are serviceable. Everyone can use a small boy."

"Kojo, I will take you." The boy's smile made me gasp. His straight white teeth clenched and I saw Bailey's smile.

"Where will you sleep?"

"Near, Auntie. Near. I have another uncle who has a place for me. But morning, I will be here. All day and evening. Thank you, Auntie. Thank you, Wofa."

He turned and ran out the screen door, slamming it behind him. I glanced at Otu quickly, hoping to catch a certain knowing look, but his face was expressionless.

Alice and Vicki accepted Kojo and within weeks he seemed a part of the household. He was in the way when I wanted to cook, in the living room dusting furniture which Otu had just polished, sitting in my parked car playing with the steering wheel and smiling, always smiling that Bailey smile.

"Auntie," Otu was helping me prepare dinner.

"Otu."

"Auntie, that small boy, Kojo, wants to speak to you."

"Well? He speaks to me all the time."

"He thought, Auntie, that he would speak to you after dinner."

I suppose I should have known that something important was coming, but I did not.

Alice and Vicki were out and I was sitting drinking Nestlé's coffee in an easy chair when Kojo whispered from the dining room, "Auntie, is it time to talk to you now?"

"Come in, Kojo, don't hang about out there."

He stood a few steps from me, his head bowed.

"Kojo, look at me. Don't pretend shyness. I know you."

"Auntie." The sweet smile and soft voice were softening me for whatever was to come.

"Auntie, you see, I am a small boy." Everyone could see that.

"And I need to go to school."

Of course. How could I have not noticed that summer was ending and he would have to return to his village?

"Yes, Kojo. Certainly you need an education. When will you be leaving?"

"Well, Auntie, the school I want is here, in Accra, just near to this place." He waited and my brain laboriously began to work. He wanted me to send him to school and to pay his fees. I had been set up.

"Auntie, I have my school fees and they have accepted me. Only I want to continue to be your small boy." Again I had misjudged the child. He was not manipulating me. He liked me. I let him know of my relief.

"Well, of course, Kojo, if you are able to do your school work and still be my small boy, you are welcome. I like you too, Kojo." When he left we were both smiling broadly.

Two weeks later he brought a letter addressed to me. The headmaster asked for my presence to discuss Kojo's courses. The meeting was so long and detailed I was exhausted when I finally arrived late at the university. Kojo had brought good grades from his village school, but he had not studied certain required subjects. The headmaster explained that the boy would need a great deal of help at home and he was so lucky to have educated Aunties.

Three evenings each week, Alice, Vicki or I sat with Kojo at the dining table conjugating verbs, dividing sums and making maps to scale.

At times an annoying thought would buzz in my head; my son was finally grown up and at college. While packing his clothes for the university, I included my last nights of poring over homework and worrying about grades. I locked into his cases the years of concentrating over childish penmanship and memorizing the capitals of countries and their chief exports. I had been freed. Now, with Kojo's eagerness the old became new and I was pinched back into those familiar contractions. His young laughter, high-pitched and honest, and his resemblance to Bailey enchanted me away from resistance. I resumed the teaching-mother role automatically and easily, save for the odd uncomfortable moment when I felt trapped in a déjà vu.

The music of the Fanti language was becoming singable to me, and its vocabulary was moving orderly into my brain.

Efua took me to a durbar, a thanksgiving feast in Aburi, about thirty miles from Accra. Thousands of gaily dressed celebrants had gathered, waving, singing and dancing. I stood on the edge of the crowd to watch the exotic parade. Hunters, rifles across their shoulders, marched in rhythm to their own drummers. Soldiers, with faces set in grim determination, paced down the widened roads behind their drummers while young girls screamed approval. Farmers bearing scythes and fishermen carrying nets were welcomed loudly by the throng.

The annual harvest ritual gave each segment in the society its opportunity to thank God and to praise its workers and their yield.

I was swaying to the rhythm when the drums stopped, and the crowd quieted. The restless air steadied. A sound, unlike the other sounds of the day, commenced in the distance. It was the harsh tone of hundreds of giant cicadas grinding their legs together. Their rasping floated to us and the crowd remained quiet but edgy with anticipation. When men appeared out of the dust scraping sticks against corrugated dry gourds, the crowd recovered its tongue.

"Yee! Yee! Awae! Awae!"

The scrapers, like the paraders who preceded them, gave no notice to the crowd or to the small children who ran unceremoniously close to their serried ranks.

Rasp, Rasp. Scrape! Scrape, Scour, Scrunch, Scrump. Rasp, Rasp! Scree! The raspers faded into a dim distance.

The deep throb of royal drums was suddenly heard in the distance and again the din of celebration stopped. The people, although quiet again, continued to move, sidle, exchange places and wipe their brows. Women adjusted the clothes which held babies securely to their backs. Rambunctious children played tag, men and women waved at each other, smiled, but kept looking toward the sound of the drums.

Efua touched my shoulder and offered me a large white handkerchief.

I said, "Thank you, but I'm all right." She kept her hand extended. I took the handkerchief.

Men emerged out of the dim dust. One set had giant drums hefted onto their shoulders, and others followed in splendid cloth, beating the drums with crooked sticks. The powerful rhythms rattled my bones, and I could feel the vibrations along the edges of my teeth.

People began clapping, moving their feet, their hands, hips and heads. They shouted clamorously, "Yee! Yee! Aboma!" And there was still a sense of anticipation in the turbulence. They were waiting for a climax.

When the first palanquin hove into view, I thought of a Chinese junk on the Yangtze (which I had never seen), and a ten ton truck on a California freeway (which I knew well). Long poled hammocks, sturdy as Conestogas, were carried by four men. In the center of each conveyance sat a chief, gloriously robed in rich hand-woven Kente cloth. At his side (only a few chiefs were female) sat a young boy, called the Kra, who, during an earlier solemn ceremony, had received the implanted soul of the chief. If the chief should die during the ritual, there would be no panic, for his people would know that his soul was safe in the young boy's body and, with the proper ritual, could be placed into the body of the chief's successor.

The drums beckoned, the kings appeared, and the air nearly collapsed under the weight of dust and thudding drums and shouting jubilation.

Each chief was prouder than the one preceding him. Each dressed in more gold and richer colors. Each black beyond ebony and shining with oil and sweat. They arrived in single file to be met by the adoring shouts of their subjects. "Na-na. Na-na." "Yo, Yo, Nana." The shouting united with the thumping of the drums and the explosion of color. Women and men bounced up and down like children's toys, and children not tall enough to see over the crowd were lifted by the nearest adults to see their passing royalty.

A flutter of white billowed over that excited scene. Thousands of handkerchiefs waving from thousands of black hands tore away my last reserve. I started bouncing with the entranced Ghanaians, my handkerchief high above my head, I waved and jumped and screamed, "Na-na, na-na, na-na."

The sunlit dance floor seethed with wiggling bodies. Benson's High Life Orchestra played the popular tune "Wofa No, No." After dancing for a half hour, I was resting at my table in preparation for another spree. On Ghana's dance floors, women and men could dance alone or with members of the same sex without causing the slightest notice. As I looked around at the mostly empty tables, I saw a man in a white lace Grand Bou Bou whose size was startling. His back was turned so his face was not visible, but he sat so high above the surface of his table he had to be over six and a half feet tall. He had broad shoulders and a very thick neck.

I didn't want to be caught staring if he turned, but I did

cut my eyes in his direction often, hoping to see his face. When the orchestra finished playing, three women and a small man returned, laughing, to his table. The big man stood and roared, "Bienvenue. C'était bien?" He turned and I saw that his face had the regularity of a perfect square. Every feature was of the proper size and in the proper place. He looked like romantic drawings of ancient African kings on caparisoned horses. He would have been at home surrounded by voluminous tents, talking birds and camel caravans. He remained standing while the women sat. He pulled the smaller man away from the table and bent his great bulk to speak privately and briefly. When he finished he spoke to the women and they gathered their stoles and purses and followed him as he made a path through the tables to the door. I watched the small man walk toward my table. In a wee corner of my mind I hoped that he was headed for a destination beyond me.

He stopped and gave me a slight bow. "Mademoiselle?"

I nodded.

"May I take a little of your time?"

I nodded again. He sat nicely on the edge of a chair.

"My name is Mamali, and I have a friend." His quiet voice and manner gave him a ministerial air.

"Yes?"

"May I ask your name and if you are married?"

My answers were as direct as his questions.

"Is it possible that you noticed the large man who sat at that table?"

I reined in wild horses and answered with calm dignity, "I noticed him."

"He is my friend. He is Sheikhali, and he has asked me to ask you if you will dine with him tonight." He took out a note pad and pen.

The horses were surging again. I said, "But I don't know him. Who is he? Where does he live? Where would we dine?"

"Miss Angelou, he is from Mali. He imports thorough-bred horses and was formerly the largest importer of beef to Ghana. When he visits Accra for business purposes, he generally stays at my residence, but he has a place and I am certain that he would take you to a very fine restaurant."

"But is he married?" He had treated the three laughing women with the indulgence of a benevolent Pasha.

Mamali looked up from his note pad, "All personal questions must be directed to himself. If you agree to dine, I will need your address. He will come for you at nine o'clock."

I hoped that I wasn't accepting too quickly, but how could one know the peculiarities of a culture glimpsed largely in a technicolor fantasy?

My disappointment at finding the house empty was enormous. I needed Alice and Vicki to counsel me on what to wear. I needed to share my excitement over Sheikhali and most crucial, I needed them to see him and let him see them. Suppose he kidnapped me and sold me to an Arab trader? My apprehension was not bootless. During my stay in Cairo I knew ambassadors from sub-Saharan Africa who rushed to Arab countries to negotiate for the release of their nationals stolen and placed for sale on the still active slave market.

It was most important that Sheikhali see my friends and understand that they were intelligent, worldly Americans who could call out the American Army to rescue me. When that last idea came to me I had been searching my closet for an elegant, rich but simple dress. I stopped and sat on the bed, imagining the American government, which had been a participant in both my people's enslavement and emancipation, sending troops to rescue me from one more auction block.

At the knock I opened the door and my knees weakened. Sheikhali filled up the whole outdoors. He wore yards of blue silk embroidered with real gold, a small blue lace cap draped itself jauntily over his brow.

"Miss Angelou?"

"Please come in."

His presence ate up every inch of space, and there was hardly any air left for me to breathe.

I said calmly, "Please sit down. My friends will be here soon."

He sat, stretching long legs out into the center of the room.

"Your ... uh ... friends? ... Your friends to eat? You, me, restaurant?"

His English was terrible. I asked in French, if he would prefer to speak French.

When Sheikhali smiled, I knew I had earned one more star for my heavenly crown. His black lips opened gradually and his teeth shone as diamonds spied through the darkness of a deep pocket.

"You speak French, too?" He used the familiar "tu," and I was pleased.

I explained that I wanted to let my friends know where I was going and with whom. He nodded, the smile still on his face. "Write them a note. Tell them Sheikhali is taking you to L'Auberge Restaurant in his avion d'argent."

Ghanaians called the 1963 Coupe de Ville Cadillac with its high standing fins and prohibitive cost "money with wings," so I was not surprised to hear Sheikhali call his car a silver airplane. I wrote two notes for my housemates, and allowed the gallant caliph to usher me into his silver American chariot.

In the restaurant he waved away the waiter and the menu and spread his hands like large palmetto fans on the tablecloth.

He spoke to me, "We will have coquille St.-Jacques, trout, and beef steak. I suppose you drink wine?" I hesitated. Clearly he was not used to dissent. In the car I had been as demure as an African violet, but now I had to speak. I said, "Thank you, but I don't eat fish or seafood. I'd like steak and vegetables." A tinge of surprise widened his eyes, then he smiled.

"American women. It is said that you know much. I see you (again the familiar 'tu') know what you will and will not eat. And wine, will wine please you?"

As a Muslim, he was not supposed to drink alcohol. I refused the wine. His look was piercing.

He clapped his hands and the waiter scurried to his side.

"Mademoiselle will have steak, vegetables and wine. Good wine." He continued ordering his own meal. I looked around the restaurant, trying not to think about the man or the rest of the evening and my good or bad luck at catching his attention.

"Mademoiselle Angelou," his voice was a soft rumble, "May I call you Maya?" He was already using "tu," so I said yes, and he took the conversation by force.

Although he often visited France he had never been to the States, and was it true that after slavery White Americans gave their money to the Blacks and now all Blacks were rich? I don't think he heard my gasped denial. And why wasn't I married? I was tall and young and pretty. Had all the men in Ghana gone blind? I murmured

against the flattery, but he touched my hand very gently,
"Don't you want children? You must not wait long, for a
woman can live without a husband, but everyone must
have at least one child." He was obviously concerned.

"I have a son."

"In America?"

"No, my son is here at the university." He was too dignified to display his surprise, but I saw the flicker cross his
face.

"You have a child at the university, but then how old
are you?" I said, "I'll tell you my son's age. He is eighteen.
But my mother says a woman who will tell her own age
will tell anything." For the first time, I heard him laugh.
He slapped his leg and nodded approval.

"I like a funny woman. Pretty women are seldom
funny. I like you." And I liked him. He was certainly the
most sublimely handsome man I had ever seen. I knew
that if the purple was visible in his blue-black skin under
artificial light, he would be stunning in direct sunlight.

I asked, "Tell me about yourself. Everything but your
age."

He smiled, and as I drank wine he told me of his youth.

He was the first son of a fourth wife. His father, who
sired thirty-two children, had given most of his attention
to the first sons. He had married Sheikhali's mother, the
youngest wife, in his old age. She had been catered to and
petted by her husband and all his wives because she had
brought a whisper of youth back to the aging man, but
after Sheikhali's birth, the old man sickened and died,
and nearly all his goods had been shared by the older
wives and their offspring.

When he was ten years old, he joined other young men
and began herding cattle. They walked cows and goats
through rain forests, across the savannahs, and over the

desert, protecting them from wild animals, venomous snakes, and severe weather. By thirteen, after his initiation into manhood, he was made leader of the drive and became sole supporter of his mother, her mother and family.

I told him, "I compliment you. You've had a hard youth, but now you have become a rich man."

"I was a man at thirteen. I am still a man. Nothing has changed."

Maybe it was that balance of maleness and manliness which intrigued me. I had long known that there were worlds of difference between males and men as there were between females and women. Genitalia indicated sex, but work, discipline, courage and love were needed for the creation of men and women.

Dinner was finished and I couldn't remember the taste of anything I had eaten.

"Now, we go to the hotel." He clapped his hands again.

I tensed. How dare he assume that he could take me to dinner and then immediately to bed. I was no prude and the thought of those large arms around me did make my breath quicken, but I needed some soft talk, some endearments, a few "honeys" and "darlings."

He pulled a tooled leather bag from his smock and gave bills to the waiter.

"For you. Now help the mademoiselle." The waiter pulled my chair and when I stood I saw Sheikhali was already at the door. He could hurry all he wanted, I followed idly, selecting the best way to reject an invitation which had not yet been offered.

We were in the car before any apt words came to me. Just as I formed a disclaiming and apologetic sentence, he began to sing. The tone was naturally deep and the melody haunting. I didn't understand the words, but the meaning was clear.

I was being serenaded. Possibly in his culture a serenade was equal to an evening of sweet talk and all the blandishments one could wish.

He parked at the Continental Hotel, and helped me out of the car.

"This is the best dance band in Accra, but if you prefer we can go on to the Star Hotel. Benson is playing there tonight."

I shook my head and he took the gesture to mean I didn't choose the Star Hotel. In fact, I was physically responding to my ignorance. He had mentioned hotel, and I had immediately assumed that he was planning an erotic tryst and had just talked myself out of and into agreement.

I didn't have to act demure when we entered the lobby. Embarrassment had made me truly docile. Sheikhali laughed when he danced and oh, the man could move. He lifted his arms and yards of blue silk billowed. He spun around and the lights glinted off the gold threads. His cap, still on his head, was the only non-moving part of the whirling mountainous man. Years of dance classes and professional dancing did not allow me to keep pace with Sheikhali. At the end of the first song he glided close and gathered me in his arms.

"You move like a night wind. A soft night wind. I like you."

We spent hours dancing and looking at each other. He whispered a translation of the song he had sung in the car: "A man loved a woman for her large eyes, for her hair that moved like a hive of bees, for her hands and sweet voice. And she answered him with a promise of eternal faithfulness." When he clapped his hands and drew out his money pouch, I was sorry the evening was over.

"We can go to the Star Hotel if you like, or I can take you home." He looked down at me from an enormous height. "Or since I have an apartment in this hotel, we can go there and rest for a time."

Happily, I chose the apartment.

Sheikhali was exotic, generous and physically satisfying, but we had trouble translating ourselves to each other. My upbringing had not fitted me for even a pretended reticence. As a Black American woman, I could not sit with easy hands and an impassive face and have my future planned. Life in my country had demanded that I act for myself or face terrible consequences.

Three days after our meeting, I returned home to find a grinning Kojo and a large white refrigerator standing in my living room.

Kojo rubbed the enamel and said, "Auntie, it's for you."

"For me? From where?"

"Briscoe's, Auntie. It came today." He grinned. Admiring me as much as the refrigerator. "The Mali man sent it."

I read the tag attached to the door of the appliance. *"For Mrs. Maya Angelou. From Mr. Sheikhali."* I said, "But I have a refrigerator."

"I know, Auntie, but the Mali man said you could have two."

"It's silly. I'll send it back." Consternation wiped away Kojo's grin. "Oh, Auntie. You'll hurt the Mali man."

"Tomorrow I will call Briscoe's and have someone come here and pick it up. Nobody has enough food for two refrigerators."

"But please, Auntie." He was pleading as if he was the donor, or even worse the recipient.

"I will do so, tomorrow." His little shoulders fell and he turned, mumbling, and walked into the kitchen.

That next evening Kojo met me at the door.

"Auntie, Briscoe came and got your refrigerator." His voice accused. He shook his head sadly. "Poor Mister Mali man."

Sheikhali was disappointed that I refused his gift, but he offered to pay my rent and give me money for my car. When I explained that I was a woman used to working and paying my own bills, he stared at me in a questioning silence.

One late evening, in his hotel room, he told me he would marry me and take me to Mali. I would learn his language, Fufulde, and teach his children proper French and English.

"What children? You have children?" I was standing at the window, looking down on the lighted gardens.

"I have eight children, from two women. But only one wife. You will like her. She is a good woman. Tall like you." He sat on the bed, looking like a black Buddha, his wide shoulders outlined by a white sleeveless undershirt.

"You will be my second wife. I will build you a beautiful house and you will be happy."

The unusual proposal nearly made me laugh.

"But if you have one wife who is good, why do you want to marry me? And you already have children. What do you want with me?"

I sat beside him on the bed.

"If I need more children I will take a young girl because you and my wife will have no more babies. But you, you are kind and educated. My wife is also kind, but she is like me, she has no education. My family will accept you. I will send to America for your parents and I will bring your son to Mali. Thus our families will marry."

He had taken my life and the lives of my entire family, except my brother, into his plan. There was no way to explain that not one of us could live within his embrace. He laughed when I thanked him, but refused.

"Women always say no. I will find out what you want, and then I will ask again."

My emotions, raised on the romance of Hollywood films, might have faltered had he pleaded love, but his offer had the crispness of a business negotiation, and I had no difficulty in refusing to participate in the transaction.

Kojo had been my "small boy" for two months. He had settled into his school routine and was usually available for small chores and swift errands.

"Auntie?" His downcast eyes and softened voice made me tense. He wanted something. "Kojo, what is it now?" Clothes? Shoes? A new school?"

"Auntie, there are some people to see you." He stayed so far beyond the door only a quarter of his body was visible.

"People? Where? What do they want?"

He whispered, "In the backyard, Auntie."

No visitor had ever come to my back door. I hurried through the kitchen and opened the screen. The yard was filled with people dressed in rich cloth and gold. A very old man, leaning on a carved stick, was surrounded by two middle-aged couples, some young adults, and a few teenagers.

A middle-aged man spoke, "Good afternoon, Auntie. We would speak to you." I reproached Kojo for allowing the people to stand in the backyard, and said to the man, "Thank you. Kojo will take you around to the front. Please come inside."

Kojo giggled, and keeping his eyes down, slithered around me and out into the yard.

I went back through the house and opened the door. The people filed into the living room, each shaking my hand and murmuring a name I couldn't quite comprehend. I offered the available chairs, and the older people sat leaving one chair for me. The younger visitors remained standing. I had no idea what the occasion was, but the formality of my visitors was clearly ritualistic.

I called Kojo to bring beer. When one woman complimented me on the prettiness of the living room, the crowd agreed quietly. A man admired a Kofi Bailey print of Kwame Nkrumah which hung on a far wall. There were faint approving sounds "Osagyefo." "Man pass man."

After the beer was served and Kojo left the room, the old man cleared his throat.

"Auntie, we have come to thank you for Kojo. We are his family. These are his brothers and sisters." The teenagers bobbed and smiled. "His uncles and aunts are here and there is his mother and his father. I am the great-grandfather of Kojo, and we thank you."

The family was nodding and smiling. I looked toward the kitchen door, expecting to catch a glimpse of a peeping Kojo, but there was none.

The old man continued, "We have come by lorry from Akwapim, and we have brought thanks."

By their bearing, clothes and jewelry, it was evident that Kojo's family was high-born and well-to-do. If they had travelled from Akwapim by lorry to thank me, it was also clear that they treasured the boy.

"Speak, Mother." Great-grandfather stretched his hand to a woman sitting to his right.

"Auntie," the woman was twice my age. "The boy, Kojo, is good and he might become better. All the mothers cherish him." Here the women gave an amen corner response. "He has grown in our family and in our village, so he was sent to the town. And proof of his goodness is he found you and your Sisters." A new rumble of agreement trembled in the room.

The old man stretched his hand to a tall man who resembled Kojo. "Speak, Father."

"Auntie, we have family here in the town, but none has the Brioni education." In Akan languages Brioni meant White. "Our chief and our grandfather told us if Kojo was to become better, he must have that understanding. Now we have talked to his headmaster. We have spoken to his teachers, and we have listened to your steward who is our cousin. Without payment and without knowing his family, you, Auntie, and your Sisters are teaching our Kojo the Brioni ways of thinking, and so . . ." His voice trailed away.

The old man spoke. "Bring the thanks."

The lounging teenagers came away from the wall. The older repeated, "Bring the thanks." When they walked out, I smiled, but could think of nothing to say, and since none of the Ghanaians I had met indulged in small talk, it wasn't surprising that the room became quiet. I was not immodest enough to think we deserved thanks, and I knew my housemates would be embarrassed when I related the episode. I kept smiling. The youngsters brought in a crate of vegetables, then another and another, and it seemed they would never stop. They packed crates against crates until the floor was covered.

The old man pointed to a box of eggplant. "Here are garden eggs. Here onions, plantain, pineapples, cassava, yam, coco yam, mango, paw paw, and outside in ice we have brought you snails." He meant the land mollusk which was as large as a kitten and which even starvation could not force down my throat. My jaws ached from smiling.

He continued, "We want you to know that Kojo did not come from the ground like grass. He has risen like the banyan tree. He has roots. And we, his roots, thank you."

The old man braced his cane against the floor and pulled himself nearly erect. The other visitors and I arose.

"Kojo's family has many farms, Auntie." That was obvious. "And while we are not trying to repay you and your Sisters, every month we will send you thanks according to the season."

Each person shook my hand and filed out of the house.

The grin on my face had become painfully permanent, and I grinned until I watched Kojo bouncing in the street before his adoring family. They patted him, brushed his clothes, stroked his face, all talking at once. I waited behind the screen until they bade their final good-byes and left him looking like a forlorn puppy against the fence.

"Kojo." He jumped and turned to me.

"Kojo, come this instant."

The boy walked to the house, trying without immediate success to exchange the intoxicating security of being loved with his usual disguise of the befuddled youth. By the time he reached the door and opened the screen, he was timid, young Kojo, my small boy and servant.

"Kojo, why didn't you tell me?"

"Tell you what, Auntie?"

It would sound silly to reproach the boy for not telling me that he had family and that his family was wealthy. And even more stupid, to blame him for being loved.

I lied. "Why didn't you tell me that your family was coming?"

"Oh that, Auntie? I knew they would come someday. I just didn't know when." He looked at me out of Bailey's eyes and grinned. "Auntie, after I take these thanks to the kitchen, may I make you some tea? White tea with lots of sugar?"

"Yes, thank you, Kojo." The visit had been brief but arduous. I had been taken further on my search for Africa and, at least, I had grinned throughout the entire journey.

"Yes, Kojo, I would love some tea with milk, no sugar." I had a half bottle of gin under my bed. Gin with hot tea was just what I needed.

I lay on my bed drinking for myself and for all the

nameless orphans of Africa who had been shunted around the world.

I drank and admitted to a boundless envy of those who remained on the continent, out of fortune or perfidy. Their countries had been exploited and their cultures had been discredited by colonialism. Nonetheless, they could reflect through their priests and chiefs on centuries of continuity. The lowliest could call the name of ancestors who lived centuries earlier. The land upon which they lived had been in their people's possession beyond remembered time. Despite political bondage and economic exploitation, they had retained an ineradicable innocence.

I doubted if I, or any Black from the diaspora, could really return to Africa. We wore skeletons of old despair like necklaces, heralding our arrival, and we were branded with cynicism. In America we danced, laughed, procreated; we became lawyers, judges, legislators, teachers, doctors, and preachers, but as always, under our glorious costumes we carried the badge of a barbarous history sewn to our dark skins. It had often been said that Black people were childish, but in America we had matured without ever experiencing the true abandon of adolescence. Those actions which appeared to be childish most often were exhibitions of bravado, not unlike humming a jazz tune while walking into a gathering of the Ku Klux Klan.

I drank the gin and ignored the tea.

Ghana was flourishing. The National Council of Ghana Women, which included representatives of all the clans, was beginning to prove that centuries-old tribal mistrust could be erased with intelligence and determination. The Cacao Marketing Board reported huge profits from the country's major export. Large shining office buildings rose in the cities and the land was filled with happiness.

People stopped in the street and said to passersby, "Oh, but life is sweet, oh, and the air is cool on my skin like fresh water."

The shared joy was traceable to President Nkrumah, who had encouraged his people to cherish their African personality. His statements were memorized and repeated in the litany of teachers and students: "For too long in our history Africa has spoken through the voice of others. Now what I have called the African Personality in international affairs will have a chance of making its proper impact and will let the world know it through the voices of its sons." When he declared that West Indians and Black Americans were among Africa's great gifts to the world, the immigrant community gleamed with gratitude.

For the first time in our lives, or the lives of our remem-

bered families, we were welcomed by a president. We
lived under laws constructed by Blacks, and if we violated
those laws we were held responsible by Blacks. For the
first time, we could not lay any social unhappiness or personal failure at the door of color prejudice.

We shadowed Nkrumah's every move, and read carefully his speeches, committing the more eloquent passages
to memory. We recounted good gossip about him, loving
his name, and furiously denied all negative rumors.

Because we were still American individualists, bred in a
climate which lauded the independent character in legend
and lore, and because we had been so recently owned, we
could not be easily possessed again, therefore we tried
rather to possess the charismatic leader. His private life
belonged to us. When photos of his Egyptian wife appeared in the papers, we scanned her features and form
with a scrutiny bordering on the obsessive.

We, the Revolutionist Returnees, danced the High Life
at the Lido, throwing our hips from side to side as if we
would have no further use for them, or we would sit together over Club beer discussing how we could better
serve Ghana, its revolution and President Nkrumah. We
lived hard and dizzyingly fast. Time was a clock being
wound too tight, and we were furiously trying to be present in each giddy moment.

Then, one day the springs burst and the happy clock
stopped running. There was an attempt on the President's
life, and the spirit of Ghana was poisoned by the news.
Fortunately, the President was uninjured, but the citizens
did not escape. Makola and Bokum markets lost their
usual last-day-Mardi Gras air, and the streets were
stricken dumb. The African professors, unspeaking, sent
messages of befuddlement to each other by their sad eyes

and the shaking of their heads. Even the European faculty at Legon spoke in murmurs.

Government officials, always concerned over foreign intervention and interior espionage, were sharpened in their paranoia and began to search for spies in all corners of the country. Representatives of The Young People's Corps wrote articles, were put on the alert, and those tender faces, filled with anger and suspicion, mirrored the country's tragedy.

Some newspaper articles suggested that no true Ghanaian could possibly be involved in the scurrilous assault on the President, so obviously the search should concentrate on foreign infiltrators. Nearly all noncitizens fell under some measure of suspicion. The British, former colonial rulers, though still covertly admired, were exempt from accusations because they were considered to be mere representatives of a fading Empire.

After a few days of general inflammatory accusation, the finger of suspicion pointed toward the Soviets. Whispers and rumors suggested that those Communists, with their oblique but decided expansionist aims, had tried to kill the President in order to throw Ghana, the Light of Africa, into chaotic darkness. That swell of conjecture abated quickly. Then, the newspaper brought heady news to me. At last there were denunciations of American capitalism, American imperialism, American intervention and American racism. At last, the average Ghanaian would realize that we, the band of disenchanted Blacks, were not fabricating the tales of oppression and discrimination. Then they, not the politicians or intellectuals, they, the farmers and tradespeople and clerks and bus drivers, would stop asking us, "How could you leave America? Don't you miss your big cars?" and "Do you live in Hollywood?" Before I could really sit down and enjoy the feast of revenge, the shadow of the pointing finger moved.

A high-ranking pundit said, "America can use its Black citizens to infiltrate Africa and sabotage our struggle because the Negro's complexion is a perfect disguise. Be wary, Africa, of the Peace Corps Blacks, the AID Blacks, and the Foreign Service Blacks." He suggested finally, that Africans should approach all American Blacks with caution, "if they must be approached at all."

We saw ourselves as frail rafts on an ocean of political turbulence. If we were not welcome in Ghana, the most progressively Black nation in Africa, where would we find harbour? Naturally we sought to minimize the impact of that painful advice. A few Revolutionists joined the witch hunt, tearing away, with loud protestations, all historical ties to the newly accused. They hoped to deflect suspicion from themselves and to inch closer to the still unrealized goal of acceptance. Many of us kept silent, heads erect and eyes forward, hoping to become invisible and avoid the flaming tongues. Failing the success of that maneuver, we prayed that the assault would pass soon, leaving no scar and little memory.

As usual, I drove each day from my house in Accra to the university, seven miles away, but the distance became painfully perverse. At times, I felt I would never arrive at my destination. Roadblocks delayed progress. They were manned by suddenly mean faced soldiers, their guns threatening and unusual in a country where policemen were armed only with billy sticks. Further on the same drive, it would seem that my arrival at the University at Legon was too imminent. Before I could collect enough composure to calm my face and steady my hands, I would be on campus, where students dropped their eyes at my approach, and professors pointedly turned their backs.

As the Black American community trembled beneath the weight of unprovable innocence, the investigation progressed in all directions. Suspects were imprisoned, and rumors flew like poison arrows around the country. Some Americans and other foreigners, were deported, slowly the barbs ceased, the cacophony of distrust quieted. Life returned. The roll of drums and the sound of laughter could be heard in the streets. None of the Revolutionist Returnees had been directly accused, and we were still grateful to be in the motherland, but we had been made a little different, a little less giddy and a lot less sure.

For two weeks I worked myself into a trembling frenzy at the in-town National Theatre. While Efua directed an English translation of a Chinese play, I had helped to sew costumes and coach the student actors. I pulled and pushed the bleachers in the open air auditorium which had to be rearranged constantly. Rickety sets, made by students with no theatrical background, were ever in need of strengthening. Someone had to synchronize the taped music with the onstage action, and a person was needed in the box office. I chose to try to be all things to all the people at all times. The play's pomp and pageantry had been a great success. Ghanaians finding a similarity between the ancient Chinese spectacle and their own traditional dramas kept the theatre filled. I was shaky with exhaustion, but I held on to the idea of returning soon to the university, and that steadied me.

On a quiet Monday morning I parked my car at the Institute of African Studies and sat watching the sun light up the green lawns stretching upward to the white shining buildings. The campus was quiet. I was happy to be back in its peaceful atmosphere.

I started walking to the Faculty of Music and Dance and met Bertie Okpoku, the director of dance.

"Hey, Maya, you finally decided to come home?"

We shook hands and ended the gesture with a traditional finger snap which signified best wishes, and walked together exchanging news until I reached my office.

"Oh, yes." His face became solemn. "One bad thing happened. Sister Grace lost her whole pay packet last week." He shook his head. "Everybody in the Dance department has been affected. So don't expect much laughter around here." Grace Nuamah was the country's chief traditional dancer, a small, thick set, middle-aged woman who performed a welcoming dance at all state functions and important ceremonies. She was an Ashanti woman, with a ready smile, a soft voice, and a hilarious sense of humor. Grace supported herself, nieces and nephews, and was generous with her friends, so the news of her loss saddened my morning, and when I opened the office door and saw the desk piled a foot high with papers, I was suddenly tired. I sat down to examine the stack and it seemed that each student at Legon needed assistance of some sort, and needed me to furnish it. One student wanted a transfer, another additional financial support, while some simply needed excuses from school to take care of familial responsibilities. Each petition had to be checked against the applicant's file and the mid-morning sun was beating into my office before I noticed the passage of time.

I thought I would complete one more paper before a break. I lifted a form letter and a small brown manilla envelope caught my eye. It read, "Grace Nuamah." I opened it to find a roll of Ghanaian pounds stuffed inside. Happy surprise made me give an involuntary shout. I was living close to economic catastrophe, and I knew how precious the salary was for Grace.

She was demonstrating a dance step to her class when I entered the rehearsal hall. The students saw me first, and she, following her distraction, saw me and stopped the class. We walked together out of the door.

She said, "Sister, welcome back from the town. We missed you, oh." I said, "Sister Grace, Bertie told me about your pay—"

She interrupted, "Into each life some rain must fall." Africans whose own lore and literature are rich with proverbs also make frequent use of English axioms.

I told her that I had found something highly unusual on my desk and showed her the envelope.

She said, "But Sister, it's your pay packet." I said that my salary had been delivered to me in Accra and offered the envelope. There was not a hint of recognition on her face as she took the packet and began to read. "Well, then . . ." She narrowed her eyes against the bright sunlight. "Oh, Sister! Oh, Sister!" Stretching her arms over her head, she jumped up. "Oh, Sis-ter, Sis-ter. Hey, thank you, oh."

Students and musicians and workers, hearing her loud shouts, came running. She said in Ashanti, "Sister is blessed. She found my money. Sister is blessed." The

smiles and pats and hugs would have been worth contriv-
ing a recovery of Grace's loss.

She said, "Sister, I will repay you." I told her that I was
repaid, but she insisted. "Sister, I shall repay you."

Throughout the day, people stopped in my office to
shake my hand, rejoicing in Grace's good fortune.

Two weeks passed and the memory of the incident
waned. University life with its steady routine restored my
energies and I felt so good I decided to give myself the
treat of having a proper lunch. Like all faculty members, I
had been assigned to take meals in one of the university's
eight halls, but it was only on the rare occasion that I visited Volta Hall High Table. The dining room was vast
and tiered and quiet. Following the British academic ar-
rangement, students sat at Low Table about four feet beneath the long high row where faculty sat facing them. I
joined the members at High Table, without speaking, for
we knew each other only casually, and there was no love
lost or found between us.

Although the African food had been anglicized, it was
delicious. A Ghanaian lamb curry, cooked with a mini-
mum of spices, was served and was accompanied with
diced papaya, fresh pineapple, tomatoes and mango. I offended the steward by asking for fresh red pepper.

The steward answered with an imitative British accent,
"Oh, but Madam, we don't serve that." I knew that students brought their own pepper to the dining room and I
was also certain that the steward had had his own cache
stored in the kitchen.

When I suggested that maybe he could find a little for
me, the White professors looked at me and sniffed disapproval. So typical, their faces seemed to say. So crude a
palate and coarse a taste, so typical.

I said loudly, but with courtesy, "If you can't get some

for me, I'm sure one of the students would gladly bring
pepper to High Table." The steward frowned and reminded me of many American Negroes in the early fifties,
who were enraged whenever they saw a natural hair style
in public. They felt betrayed, as if the women wearing the
frizzy coiffure were giving away secrets; as if they were letting White folks know that our hair wasn't naturally
straight. I had seen Black people curse each other on New
York City subways and had seen women snubbed in
streets throughout the United States because they dared
to reveal their Negro-ness.

The steward, infuriated, said "I will find pepper. I will
bring pepper to you, Madam."

I ate slowly, relishing every fiery mouthful, ignoring the
departure of the faculty. Innate obstinacy made me order
and eat a dessert which I did not want and which the
steward did not wish to provide.

Coffee was served in the Senior Common Room, and I
took a seat by the window and listened to the conversation
in progress.

"It was really a little serio-comedic drama. We had
traveled about fifty miles into the interior and at nightfall
John stopped and let down the flaps of the Land Rover, so
we crawled in the back to go to sleep."

A woman's voice cut through the air, "You and the
mosquitoes, I don't doubt."

"Oh no, we had netting. Anyway, just as we were
drowsing, we heard a voice, 'Ko koko koko ko koko ko.' "

West African houses in the interior are often made of
thatch or non-resonant land-crete, so a visitor seeking entrance, unable to rap on a responding door, would politely
stand outside and make the sound of knocking, "ko ko ko,
ko ko ko."

The storyteller continued, "John lifted the flap and an

African stood there dripping wet, wearing a sarong and waving his hand at us."

At nightfall, a farmer home from his fields would take the akatado, the shawl of his wife's dress, and go to the bathhouse. After washing, the man would drape himself in cloth before returning for the evening meal.

"John made me put my slacks back on and we got out of the Rover."

One of the listeners hugged himself and chortled, "Better you than me."

The woman continued, "We didn't see that we had a choice. Anyway, we had thought we were miles from civilization, but we followed the man through a few yards of jungle and there was a village."

The same woman with the keen voice said, "Personally, wild elephants could not have made me leave that car."

"Well, the man took us to the chief, and he had someone serve us tea with whiskey in it. Pretty terrible, actually, but we drank it. Then an interpreter arrived and the old man, toothless and quite ragged, looked directly at us as he spoke his dialect."

I thought of the unpleasant irony that Africans and Asians always speak dialects, rarely languages, while Europeans speak languages and almost never dialects.

The woman continued, "The interpreter said, 'the chief says, you are human beings. I can see that, because I am a human being.' "

There was a little laughter in the Common Room.

She went on quoting the old African. " 'God made daylight so that human beings can be busy outside tending their farms, fishing, and doing all the things for which they need light. God also gave human beings this head,' " she pointed a thin finger at her own head, " 'so that they would have enough sense to make indoors. Human beings sleep indoors at night, for God made night so that animals can search for their food, and breed, and have their young.' " The woman paused, then added, "Well, I thought that was poetic. Then he sent us to a hut where ledges had been built in the walls. We were given mats to sleep on. I guess it was a kind of guest house. John said the people who had lived there before had died of mosquito bites. Anyway, we slept in our clothes and in the morning a woman was cooking over a fire just outside and she gave us yams and crab stew about seven-thirty in the morning. Imagine crab stew at seven-thirty in the morning. When we tried to give her a tip, she refused, and beckoning us to follow, took us back to the old man and the translator was called again. He stood before the chief who looked at us and shook his head as if we were naughty children. When he stopped talking, the translator said, 'The chief says "you are human beings. I can see that. God has chosen to make you without a proper skin. I do not question why. I accept. We brought you inside and slept you and fed you because you are humans. You cannot pay us. We did not make you human. God did that. You are traveling in a strange land. What less could we do? If I came to your land, and was outside, you would have to do the same for me. Could I pay you? No. For you did not make me. God did that.' "

A man with a mouthful of coffee sputtered, "Can't you just imagine the old codger caught in a revolving door in New York expecting somebody to help him because God made him?"

There was a round of self-conscious laughter.

An English woman stood, dropped her napkin and spoke in a low voice. "Even if that story is true you should never tell it again. You and your husband sound like un-grateful clods, and the African has the grace of Saint Au-gustine. I must say that I don't pity you. I don't pity Africa. I pity Europe. What poor representatives she has sent abroad. I am here to give three seminars. I must say I'll be relieved to go. You are an embarrassment."

The woman left and there was more soft embarrassed laughter. I sat watching the little group, wondering and curious to see what they would do and even more in-terested to learn what I would do.

"Well, must be going."

"I, too. See you at seven?"

"Of course."

"Ciao."

"Ta."

And they were gone. I looked at the steward, but his face had no more expression than a black billiard ball. I gathered my belongings and left the Common Room walking in an air of pleasant pride. I had not let my heart be troubled, I had not spoken idiotically, and I was over-joyed that the English woman whom I had seen only once had stood up and talked back. It was sad that she was leaving, and I wouldn't have the chance to know her.

On an early morning the small figure of a woman stood in my office door. I was used to being at the institute long before other faculty members, so I supposed the figure to be a student, but as I neared I recognized Grace Nuamah.

Her smile was white and wide and a wonderful morning treat. "Sister Maya, welcome. Sister Maya, I came early to ask you to come to lunch with me today." It wasn't yet eight o'clock. "I wanted to ask you before you made other plans. A special friend of mine is preparing food. And Sister, there will be no fish."

Grace and I left Legon under the blistering midday sun.

"Sister, I am still thanking you. We're going to Ring Road and then over to Asylum Down."

I asked whose house we were visiting. Her smile was sassy. She said, "Someone who knows how much I am in your debt. Just you wait and see."

After we reached Accra, the drive was short. Following her directions, I stopped the car in front of a large impressive house surrounded by palms and a beautifully kept flower garden. Grace laughed with happy anticipation.

"Just you wait, Sister Maya."

Her expectation was contagious, and I became excited. The door was closed, which was unusual in Ghana, and meant that the house was air conditioned.

A servant greeted us. Seeing Grace, he grinned, "Ooo, Auntie, welcome." He spoke Ashanti, so I assumed our hosts were also from the north. In the foyer, I was introduced and the servant nodded solemnly to me, but gave his smile back to Grace.

"He is expecting you, Auntie Grace. Please come and sit; I will bring beer."

We followed him into the richest living room I had seen in Ghana. Over-stuffed sofas were discreetly placed on Oriental rugs. Ornate sconces hung on walls covered with flocked paper. Crystal and silver sat on highly polished tables and recorded music issued softly into the room.

When Grace and I were alone, I asked, "Who are these folks?" Grace, still grinning, said, "Just you wait."

We were sipping beer from German steins when a side door opened and a slim man of medium height wearing a suit, shirt and tie entered the room. He moved like a dancer and spoke in a rich baritone voice.

"Oh, little Grace. So you have come. What honor you bring to my humble house."

He took Grace's hands and drew her up from the sofa. She purred like a stroked kitten. He said, "You have stayed away entirely too long. If our relationship is in jeopardy, the crime must be on your head and it is you who will pay."

He was laying it on and Grace was loving it, twisting her short body from side to side, taking one hand then the other from his grasp to put over her mouth as she smiled coquettishly. Their chatter and gestures came to an abrupt stop and Grace said, "Brother, I have brought my friend." They both turned to look at me, and I knew at once that I had been a spectator at a ritual which had been choreographed for my enjoyment.

"Sister Maya, this is my dear friend Abatanu." Now the man smiled for me. His teeth were white as if they had just been painted.

He reached for my hands and I stood.

"Miss Angelou, you have made a great impression on Grace, and she is not easily impressed. Welcome."

He held my hands a moment too long, and looked just a little too deeply into my eyes. I decided in those first moments that I didn't like his type. His suaveness was too practiced and his sophistication too professional. When he led the conversation to my background, my family, and where I lived in the States, Grace became silent, allowing us to get acquainted. Although I knew how to equivocate and to flirt by oblique responses, the man's manner so put me off that I answered politely, but directly. Only a charlatan or a fool will ignore rejection, and Mr. Abatanu was neither.

When we sat down to lunch, he spoke only to Grace, and although she repeatedly tried to include me in their conversation, he would have none of it. Grace saw her match-making intentions foiled by our mutual lack of interest, and tried every gambit to sow interest between me and my host, but at last admitting failure, we finished the meal amid awkward silences.

My departure was plain. I shook hands with Abatanu and he soberly accepted my thanks for lunch. Grace said she'd join me in the car, so I went outside and didn't have long to wait.

"Sister." Hurt and reprimand vied for prominence in her voice. "Sister," she shook her head, "Oh, Sister, and I was trying to thank you. He is a fine man, educated man, rich man, and he loves women, oh."

"Grace, I was glad to meet him, so I thank you."

"No, Sister, you didn't like him and when he saw that, he stopped liking you."

"Sister Grace, he never started liking me."

"I told you I would thank you, and you probably thought I forgot, but I have been talking to Abatanu for weeks about you, and when finally I had everything arranged you didn't like him. Oh, pity, Sister. Pity."

It was hot. I was driving and more than a little irritated that I had spent an entire afternoon bored. I said, "Sister Grace, not to be rude, but if he is so fine, why don't you have him?"

My question surprised her and drove the frown from her face. She laughed and put her hand lightly on her breast.

"Me? Me? Oh no! When you have a big beautiful gold nugget, you don't melt it down to play with it. You might lose it. A wise person puts the nugget in a strong box and saves it for an important occasion. Sister Maya, I've been saving him a long time, and I was giving him to you."

She stayed quiet for a while as I drove through heavy afternoon traffic, then she gave a great sigh and asked the breeze, "And what about him? Oh, what does he think?"

Years before I memorized a George Eliot quote, "I never feel sorry for conceited people, supposing they carry their comfort around with them." Abatanu had enough comfort to cushion him from a drop higher than the one I furnished for him. I said nothing. Grace sighed again and said, "An African woman would have appreciated the gift and accepted it."

I hadn't been expecting her to give me a teddy bear or a talking doll. I gave my attention to the highway, hurrying back to Legon. When we stopped, I got out and took

Grace's hand. "Sister, I truly appreciate your thinking so kindly of me, and I'm grateful for your generosity."

Grace would not or could not surrender her distress.

"Sister, I knew Americans were different, but. . . ." She shook her head, patted my shoulder, and I stroked her arm. We stood looking at each other with nothing more to say.

Sheikhali was late again. I had been dressed and waiting for two hours. His tardiness had become so frequent that even as I prepared for a rendezvous I did so slowly, knowing there would be no need to rush.

Our date was for seven. At nine-thirty I got into my car and drove to the Star Hotel.

The head waiter took me to a pleasant table for two, overlooking the dance floor. Hurt pride rather than hunger or my wallet made me order a bottle of wine and a three-course dinner. I had nearly finished choking down the unwanted food when Sheikhali arrived.

He wore a flowing white robe and red tasseled fez. He was followed by the small Mamali who wore a matching outfit. They strode to my table. Sheikhali called for another chair and the two men sat down.

"Maya. I went to your house. It was dark. Even the servants refused to answer." I decided not to tell him that both Otu and Kojo were away.

"I went to the Continental Hotel, the Lido, L'auberge. Am I a man to chase a woman? Look at me." Anger had furrowed his face and tightened his throat. "My French is not good enough. I have brought Mamali to speak for me."

For the first time Mamali spoke, "Good evening, Sister. Sheikhali has asked me to translate for him. He will speak Fufulde. I will translate into French."

Mamali spoke with warmth, but his posture and words were formal.

Sheikhali leaned back in his chair and looked at Mamali.

"Bon?"

Mamali nodded, the big man coughed and began. His language was melodic and his voice soft. He stopped.

Mamali said, "I have walked thousands of miles through forest storms, and I know under which tree to stand when the rains fall; a certain tree can change the mind of the winds. I know."

Mamali stopped so that Sheikhali could resume. He spoke for a long time. When his voice fell, the attentive Mamali spoke again.

"I know the desert. I find my way through sand that burns and sun that bites, and I am never lost. I look at a cow. I feed a horse. I know them. I look at the moon and read the weather. You know books. Me, I know life. I have never been into one school. Not one. You read. I can write my name. So you know schools, but I know man, woman, cow, horse, desert, jungle, sun and moon. Who is smart, you or me?"

I said nothing.

Sheikhali turned and spoke to me directly. "I will marry you, for you are a good woman. In Mali the women will teach you to be better. If you are intelligent enough, you will learn enough. Because of me, you will be respected. But you must lose this White woman way of . . ." He said a word to Mamali, who translated. "Impatience." Sheikhali continued, "Your father will come from America and we will talk." For a second I tried to imagine Bailey Johnson, Sr., who was at least as proud as Sheikhali and as stiff as a penguin, leaving his perfectly furnished home in San Diego, California, to come to Africa, which he thought was populated by savages. It was impossible to picture my fastidious father even considering a prospective son-in-law who had grown up sleeping on the ground, surrounded by cattle.

I said, "I can't marry you. I can't go to Mali. Thank you, but . . . I can't."

He turned quickly to Mamali and spoke in Fufulde. Mamali dropped his eyes. When he spoke it was with regret.

"If you say no again, I will stop trying. I am a man, not a boy to be played with. This last time, will you . . . ?"

"No. I cannot."

Sheikhali stood a mile above my head and smiled. His even teeth glistened.

"You are still a good woman, but you are not so intelligent. You are a functionaire. Only a functionaire." He spat out the words, turned and followed by Mamali, left the restaurant.

In French the word for civil servant did not sound as lifeless as in English.

Each morning Ghana's seven-and-one-half million people seemed to crowd at once into the capital city where the broad avenues as well as the unpaved rutted lanes became gorgeous with moving pageantry: bicycles, battered lorries, hand carts, American and European cars, chauffeur-driven limousines. People on foot struggled for right-of-way, white-collar workers wearing white knee-high socks brushed against market women balancing large baskets on their heads as they proudly swung their wide hips. Children, bright faces shining with palm oil, picked openings in the throng, and pretty young women in western clothes affected not to notice the attention they caused as they laughed together talking in the musical Twi language. Old men sat or stooped beside the road smoking home-made pipes and looking wise as old men have done eternally.

The too sweet aromas of flowers, the odors of freshly fried fish and stench from open sewers hung in my clothes and lay on my skin. Car horns blew, drums thumped. Loud radio music and the muddle of many languages shouted or murmured. I needed country quiet.

The Fiat was dependable, and I had a long weekend, money in my purse, and a working command of Fanti, so I decided to travel into the bush. I bought roasted plaintain stuffed with boiled peanuts, a quart of Club beer and headed my little car west. The stretch was a highway from Accra to Cape Coast, filled with trucks and private cars passing from lane to lane with abandon. People hung out of windows of the crowded mammie lorries, and I could hear singing and shouting when the drivers careened those antique vehicles up and down hills as if each was a little train out to prove it could.

I stopped in Cape Coast only for gas. Although many Black Americans had headed for the town as soon as they touched ground in Ghana, I successfully avoided it for a year. Cape Coast Castle and the nearby Elmina Castle had been holding forts for captured slaves. The captives had been imprisoned in dungeons beneath the massive buildings and friends of mine who had felt called upon to make the trek reported that they felt the thick stone walls still echoed with old cries.

The palm tree–lined streets and fine white stone buildings did not tempt me to remain any longer than necessary. Once out of the town and again onto the tarred roads, I knew I had not made a clean escape. Despite my hurry, history had invaded my little car. Pangs of self-pity and a sorrow for my unknown relatives suffused me. Tears made the highway waver, and were salty on my tongue.

What did they think and feel, my grandfathers, caught on those green Savannahs, under the baobab trees? How long did their families search for them? Did the dungeon wall feel chilly and its slickness strange to my grandmothers who were used to the rush of air against bamboo huts and the sound of birds rattling their grass roofs?

I had to pull off the road. Just passing near Cape Coast Castle had plunged me back into the eternal melodrama.

There would be no purging, I knew, unless I asked all the questions. Only then would the spirits understand that I was feeding them. It was a crumb, but it was all I had.

I allowed the shapes to come to my imagination: children passed tied together by ropes and chains, tears abashed, stumbling in dull exhaustion, then women, hair uncombed, bodies gritted with sand, and sagging in defeat. Men, muscles without memory, minds dimmed, plodding, leaving bloodied footprints in the dirt. The quiet was awful. None of them cried, or yelled, or bellowed. No moans came from them. They lived in a mute territory, dead to feeling and protest. These were the legions, sold by sisters, stolen by brothers, bought by strangers, enslaved by the greedy and betrayed by history.

For a long time, I sat as in an open-air auditorium watching a troop of tragic players enter and exit the stage.

The visions faded as my tears ceased. Light returned and I started the car, turned off the main road, and headed for the interior. Using rutted track roads, and lanes a little larger than foot paths, I found the River Pra. The black water moving quietly, ringed with the tall trees, seemed enchanted. A fear of snakes kept me in the car, but I parked and watched the bright sun turn the water surface into a rippling cloth of lamé. I passed through villages which were little more than collections of thatch huts with goats and small children wandering in the lanes. The noise of my car brought smiling adults out to wave at me.

In the late afternoon, I reached the thriving town that was my destination. A student whom I had met at Legon had spoken to me often of the gold-mining area, of Dunkwa, his birthplace. His reports had so glowed with the town's virtues, and I had chosen that spot for my first journey.

My skin color, features and the Ghana cloth I wore made me look like any young Ghanaian woman. I could pass if I didn't talk too much.

As usual, in the towns of Ghana, the streets were filled with vendors selling their wares of tinned pat milk, hot spicy Killi Willis (fried, ripe plaintain chips), Pond's Cold Cream and anti-mosquito incense rings. Farmers were returning home, children returning from school. Young boys grinned at mincing girls and always there were the market women, huge and impervious. I searched for a hotel sign in vain and as the day lengthened, I started to worry. I didn't have enough gas to get to Koforidua, a large town northeast of Dunkwa, where there would certainly be hotels, and I didn't have the address of my student's family. I parked the car a little out of the town center and stopped a woman carrying a bucket of water on her head and a baby on her back.

"Good day." I spoke in Fanti, and she responded. I continued, "I beg you, I am a stranger looking for a place to stay."

She repeated, "Stranger?" and laughed. "You are a stranger? No. No."

To many Africans only Whites could be strangers. All Africans belonged somewhere, to some clan. All Akan-speaking people belong to one of eight blood lines (Abosua) and one of eight spirit lines (Ntoro).

I said, "I am not from here."

For a second fear darted in her eyes. There was the possibility that I was a witch or some unhappy ghost from the country of the dead. I quickly said, "I am from Accra." She gave me a good smile. "Oh, one Accra. Without a home." She laughed. The Fanti word *Nkran,* for which the capitol was named, means the large ant that builds ten-foot-high domes of red clay and lives with millions of other ants.

"Come with me." She turned quickly, steadying the bucket on her head and led me between two corrugated tin shacks. The baby bounced and slept on her back, secured by the large piece of cloth wrapped around her body. We passed a compound where women were pounding the dinner foo foo in wooden bowls.

The woman shouted, "Look what I have found. One Nkran has no place to sleep tonight." The women laughed and asked, "One Nkran? I don't believe it."

"Are you taking it to the old man?"

"Of course."

"Sleep well, alone, Nkran, if you can." My guide stopped before a small house. She put the water on the ground and told me to wait while she entered the house. She returned immediately followed by a man who rubbed his eyes as if he had just been awakened.

He walked close and peered hard at my face. "This is the Nkran?" The woman was adjusting the bucket on her head.

"Yes, Uncle. I have brought her." She looked at me, "Good-bye, Nkran. Sleep in peace. Uncle, I am going." The man said, "Go and come, child," and resumed studying my face. "You are not Ga." He was reading my features.

A few small children had collected around his knees. They could barely hold back their giggles as he interrogated me.

"Aflao?"

I said, "No."

"Brong-ahafo?"

I said, "No. I am—." I meant to tell him the truth, but he said, "Don't tell me. I will soon know." He continued staring at me. "Speak more. I will know from your Fanti."

"Well, I have come from Accra and I need to rent a room for the night. I told that woman that I was a stranger . . ."

He laughed. "And you are. Now, I know. You are Bambara from Liberia. It is clear you are Bambara." He laughed again. "I always can tell. I am not easily fooled." He shook my hand. "Yes, we will find you a place for the night. Come." He touched a boy at his right. "Find Patience Aduah, and bring her to me."

The children laughed and all ran away as the man led me into the house. He pointed me to a seat in the neat little parlor and shouted, "Foriwa, we have a guest. Bring beer." A small Black woman with an imperial air entered the room. Her knowing face told me that she had witnessed the scene in her front yard.

She spoke to her husband. "And, Kobina, did you find who the stranger was?" She walked to me. I stood and shook her hand. "Welcome, stranger." We both laughed. "Now don't tell me, Kobina, I have ears, also. Sit down, Sister, beer is coming. Let me hear you speak."

We sat facing each other while her husband stood over us smiling. "You, Foriwa, you will never get it."

I told her my story, adding a few more words I had recently learned. She laughed grandly. "She is Bambara. I could have told you when Abaa first brought her. See how tall she is? See her head? See her color? Men, huh. They only look at a woman's shape."

Two children brought beer and glasses to the man who poured and handed the glasses around. "Sister, I am Kobina Artey; this is my wife Foriwa and some of my children."

I introduced myself, but because they had taken such relish in detecting my tribal origin I couldn't tell them that they were wrong. Or, less admirably, at that moment I didn't want to remember that I was an American. For the first time since my arrival, I was very nearly home. Not a Ghanaian, but at least accepted as an African. The sensation was worth a lie.

Voices came to the house from the yard.

"Brother Kobina," "Uncle," "Auntie."

Foriwa opened the door to a group of people who entered speaking fast and looking at me.

"So this is the Bambara woman? The stranger?" They looked me over and talked with my hosts. I understood some of their conversation. They said that I was nice looking and old enough to have a little wisdom. They announced that my car was parked a few blocks away. Kobina told them that I would spend the night with the newlyweds, Patience and Kwame Duodu. Yes, they could see clearly that I was a Bambara.

"Give us the keys to your car, Sister; someone will bring your bag."

I gave up the keys and all resistance. I was either at home with friends, or I would die wishing that to be so.

Later, Patience, her husband, Kwame, and I sat out in the yard around a cooking fire near to their thatched house which was much smaller than the Artey bungalow. They explained that Kobina Artey was not a chief, but a member of the village council, and all small matters in that area of Dunkwa were taken to him. As patience stirred the stew in the pot, which was balanced over the fire, children and women appeared sporadically out of the darkness carrying covered plates. Each time Patience thanked the bearers and directed them to the house, I felt the distance narrow between my past and present.

In the United States, during segregation, Black American travelers, unable to stay in hotels restricted to White patrons, stopped at churches and told the Black ministers or deacons of their predicaments. Church officials would select a home and then inform the unexpecting hosts of the decision. There was never a protest, but the new hosts relied on the generosity of their neighbors to help feed and even entertain their guests. After the travelers were settled, surreptitious knocks would sound on the back door.

In Stamps, Arkansas, I heard so often, "Sister Henderson, I know you've got guests. Here's a pan of biscuits."

"Sister Henderson, Mama sent a half a cake for your visitors."

"Sister Henderson, I made a lot of macaroni and cheese. Maybe this will help with your visitors."

My grandmother would whisper her thanks and finally when the family and guests sat down at the table, the offerings were so different and plentiful it appeared that days had been spent preparing the meal.

Patience invited me inside, and when I saw the table I was confirmed in my earlier impression. Ground nut stew, garden egg stew, hot pepper soup, kenke, kotomre, fried plantain, dukuno, shrimp, fish cakes, and more, all crowded together on variously patterned plates.

In Arkansas, the guests would never suggest, although they knew better, that the host had not prepared every scrap of food, especially for them.

I said to Patience, "Oh, Sister, you went to such trouble."

She laughed, "It is nothing, Sister. We don't want our

Bambara relative to think herself a stranger anymore. Come, let us wash and eat."

After dinner I followed Patience to the outdoor toilet, then they gave me a cot in a very small room.

In the morning I wrapped my cloth under my arms, sarong fashion, and walked with Patience to the bath house. We joined about twenty women in a walled enclosure that had no ceiling. The greetings were loud and cheerful as we soaped ourselves and poured buckets of water over our shoulders.

Patience introduced me. "This is our Bambara sister."

"She's a tall one all right. Welcome, Sister."

"I like her color."

"How many children, Sister?" The woman was looking at my breasts.

I apologized, "I only have one."

"One?"

"One?"

"One!" Shouts reverberated over the splashing water. I said, "One, but I'm trying."

They laughed. "Try hard, sister. Keep trying."

We ate leftovers from the last night feast and I said a sad good-bye to my hosts. The children walked me back to my car with the oldest boy carrying my bag. I couldn't offer money to my hosts, Arkansas had taught me that, but I gave change to the children. They bobbed and jumped and grinned.

"Good-bye, Bambara Auntie."

"Go and come, Auntie."

"Go and come."

I drove into Cape Coast before I thought of the gruesome castle and out of its environs before the ghosts of slavery caught me. Perhaps their attempts had been half-hearted. After all, in Dunkwa, although I let a lie speak for me, I had proved that one of their descendants, at least one, could just briefly return to Africa, and that despite cruel betrayals, bitter ocean voyages and hurtful centuries, we were still recognizable.

The worthy Otu dropped his customary aplomb and rushed nimbly into the kitchen.

He whispered, "Madame, Nana's driver is here. Madame, I didn't know you knew Nana. His driver has come to get you. He is waiting in the car. It's Nana's Mercedes outside."

He was shaken by excitement and awe and the dual assault made him accusatory.

He peered discourteously into my face, "Madame," [the friendly title "Auntie" was forgotten] "do you know the Nana?"

"Yes." I gave him the answer dryly, shielding my own surprise.

One evening, months before, I had met the chief at Efua's house and had spoken to him about Guy's entrance into the university.

Although Conor Cruise O'Brien was then head of the University of Ghana, Nana Nketsia had been the first

African Vice Chancellor, stepping down for O'Brien at his own decision.

The Ghanaian academic system, following its British model, accepted students who had completed a Sixth Form, which was equal to an American two-year junior college course. Guy had only completed high school, but I explained to the Nana that at home he would be qualified to enter our best institutions. My argument, assisted by the pathos of a mother appealing for a sick and hospitalized son, won the day.

Weeks later I was informed that Guy would be accepted if he passed an entrance examination. I had not seen the Nana since that first meeting, but I had heard much about him. He was an Ahanta Paramount Chief who, in ancient times, would have had absolute power. The modern Nana was fiercely political. He had been the first Ghanaian chief to be arrested for resisting British colonialism and had been educated in Britain, coming down from Oxford with double firsts, equal to the American summa cum laude. He was an adviser to President Nkrumah and Ambassador Plenipotentiary. Along with those staggering credits, Nana was handsome.

If Otu was shocked by the unheralded appearance of the Chief's driver, I was stunned.

I waged a small war in my closet, selecting and rejecting what was to be worn to a chief's house. As I walked outside, Otu, who had become a stranger, stood at sharp attention, his arms at his side, his eyes down.

"Good evening, Madame." As if I didn't have sufficient nervousness, he transferred his tension to me, and I barely greeted the driver who held the car door open.

The drive was too short to clear my mind. I had never been face to face with royalty and didn't know the protocol. I suspected that I had been sent for to discuss some incident pertaining to the presence of Black American residents, and I was nervous. I knew I was given to dramatic overstatement, or was known to waffle about repetitiously. To further complicate matters, I was sincere. Sincerity badly stated elicits mistrust.

The driver stopped before a mansion, which in the dark, surrounded by even darker trees, appeared ominous. Light came from a few windows, and the small fires of servants were visible in the compound beyond the house. Muffled drums could be heard from a distant hill. I noticed only a few cars parked along the street when I got out of the car. I asked the driver if the Nana was giving a party.

He shook his head and gave me an impish smile. "Auntie, I do not hear your language."

The driver opened the front door for me and I walked into a woodland fantasy.

The large living room was furnished with rich sofas, burl tables and was interrupted by a wide-branched tree that grew up through the ceiling. African mats were thrown on the tiled floor, and in a distant corner two men sat talking under lamp light.

The chauffeur disappeared after he ushered me through the door, and the men seemed to take no notice of me. I stood unsure in the shadows and struggled with a decision. What was the proper way to address a chief, and more hazardous, what would he think of me if I violated some unknown but sacred taboo?

In Egypt I had seen well-dressed and urbane diplomats prostrate themselves before a visiting Hausa chief, and I had read that the Akan chiefs were believed to be the living embodiment of all the Fantis and Ashantis who had ever lived; therefore, their leaders' physical bodies were sacred.

Admittedly, my ancestors had come from Africa, but I was my own person from St. Louis, Arkansas and California, a member of a group which had successfully held a large and hostile nation at bay. Anyway, I had been minding my own business in my own house. I hadn't asked to come to pay homage to anybody.

I walked past the tree over the slippery mats and into the light.

"Nana? I am Maya Angelou. You sent for me?"

Both men looked up and their smiles were quick. They had been aware of my entrance and of my hesitation all along.

"Miss Angelou. Welcome to my home. Please meet Mr. Kwesi Brew." The chief wore a white Northern Territory smock. His black skin, white teeth and red tongue made for an unutterable drama.

Kwesi Brew rose and shook my hand. I had read his lyrical poetry and knew that he was Minister of Protocol in charge of State formalities, so I was not prepared for his boyishness.

"Sister, so I am getting to meet the very famous Maya Angelou. Too many people in the country say good things of you. Can you be that good?"

"Mr. Brew, I am happy. It is always a pleasure to meet a poet."

He was caught off-guard, but recovered in an instant. "Oh, Miss Angelou, you don't mean you have wasted time reading my sad little efforts?"

"Mr. Brew, I am certain that your poem, 'If this is the time to conquer my heart, do so now,' is neither little nor is it sad."

A delighted laugh popped out of his mouth. "Oh, oh, Nana. This one! This lady. But she's quick, oh!"

Nana nodded, smiling, "Kwesi, sit. Maya. May I call you Maya?" I nodded.

"Maya, sit. Welcome to the Ahenfie. That means the house of the Nana, and what will you have to drink?"

I said I had no preference, and he shook his head. "A woman like you should always have a preference." I thought of my grandmother. If I responded to a question of choice by saying, "I don't care," she would give me a look identical to the one I had just seen on Nana's face. Then she would warn me that "Don't care ain't got no home."

I told Nana, "I'll have gin and ginger." He said, "You can have schnapps. Schnapps is the proper drink for serious conversation." Immediately I drew up, stiffened my spine. "I'm sorry, I don't drink schnapps. If you don't have gin and ginger, I will have water."

Kwesi laughed, "Oh, Nana, I had better be your Ocheame." He turned to me still smiling, but with a formal air. "Sister, anything you want to say to the Nana, say it to me. I will be your correspondent. Speak only to me." He had the posture and only needed the livery to be taken for the chief's spokesman.

"Please, Ocheame, I would like to have a schnapps. It is good for me." Nana smiled, acknowledging my tact, and called for drinks.

I had never heard such a voice. In ordinary conversation it had been deep and mellifluous, but raised to a shout, it rattled and clattered and clanged like a cowbell played by a madman.

*"Kwame, take whiskey and bring it."* He shouted, or yelled in Fanti, and I imagined that every mote of dust in the

room quivered into action. I must have jumped because Kwesi put his hand on my arm and grinned. "My chief's got some voice, huh?"

When drinks were placed before us, Nana poured a libation on the tiles and said a prayer to the old ones. It was done as perfunctorily as grace is said at an informal family table. He drank first then in an ordinary voice he said, "Maya, we have been talking about the Afro-Americans. Osagefo knows America. He said that in the United States he was not an African from the Gold Coast. Whites only saw the color of his skin and treated him like a nigger."

Kwesi added, "Aggrey of Africa also lived in the United States for a while. You know who he was, don't you, Sister?"

Nana intruded, "Dr. Kwegyr Aggrey from Ghana earned a doctorate from Columbia University and taught in North Carolina. He understood racism and he loved his Black skin. He said, 'If I died and went to heaven and God asked me would I like to be sent back to earth as a White man' "—Nana's voice was thundering again—" 'I would say no, make me as Black as you can and send me back.' " The klaxon trumpeted. "Aggrey of Africa said, 'Make me completely Black, BLACK, BLACK.' "

That was the spectacular language, the passion of self-appreciation. I had traveled to Africa to hear it, and hear in an African voice, and in such a splendor of sound.

The gold chain on the chief's black chest was cruelly bright. "Aggrey speaks for me. Aggrey speaks for Africa. We are Black, BLACK! And we give no explanation, no apology."

The warmth flowed through me and I had to hold on, close my teeth, contract my muscles or I would have become an embarrassing quiver of gratitude.

Kwesi Brew lifted his glass. "I propose a toast, Nana. A toast." He bounded up and I quickly stood to clink his glass. I expected Nana to join us, but the chief remained seated, although he held his glass aloft.

Kwesi said, "To the African Personality." I gestured with my glass and repeated, "To the African Personality." Nana roared, "To the African Personality," and we drank.

I realized that I had not seen the tribal leader on his feet since my arrival. His bare muscled arms were robust and his skin was as smooth as black flannel, but maybe he was ill.

Kwesi saw my concern and shook his head, "Sister, Nana does not stand. In our tradition everyone stands for the Nana, but the Nana, spiritual and moral leader of Ahanta people, stands for no one. It would mean that all the Ahantas are standing and no one is great enough to command such tribute, you understand? Na Na. Ena ena. Mother of his people, father of his country."

The chief busied himself during that explanatory speech. He twisted the knobs on the radio at his side and sipped from his glass of schnapps.

"But Sister"—Kwesi poured drinks for the two of us— "We, you and I, are lowly mortals, not saints like our chief."

Nana roared a cautionary "Kwesi," and Kwesi laughed. "Nana, you are my chief, and if I make a mistake I am certain you will overlook it." Nana smiled and beckoned Kwesi to sit down again.

He spoke in a moderate voice, "You are my poet, and maybe Ocheame, but you are not my jester. Sit, now and let me talk more to this lady."

Kwesi and I sat obediently upon the sofas like scolded children.

"Efua speaks of you as a sister. T. D. Bafoo, our enfant terrible, claims you are his relative. Even Kofi Batcha and others supported your membership in the Ghana Press Club. Julian Mayfield was the only Black American there until you came."

Nana listed each commendation as if he were reading from a plaque soon to be presented to me.

He continued, "It is known that your salary at the University is less than any amount paid to a non-Ghanaian. It is also known that your son studies at Legon and that you receive no financial assistance for his education."

His monologue was leading toward a sweet haven of help. I knew now why I had been sent for. The Chief and the Chief of Protocol were about to announce that I had been allotted a fabulous raise. A smile slipped out of my control, but Nana was not watching me, and Kwesi, who had not taken his gaze from my face, smiled back. "You are a mother and we love our mothers." Nana had reached a rhythm reminiscent of preachers in Southern Black churches. There would be no turning back.

"Africa is herself a mother. The mother of mankind. We Africans take motherhood as the most sacred condition human beings can achieve. Camara Laye, our brother, has said, 'The Mother is there to protect you. She is buried in Africa and Africa is buried in her. That is why she is supreme.' "

Kwesi was accompanying Nana with his voice, "Ka, Nana, Ka, Nana, Ka, Nana."

I had been forgotten for the while as the men performed a concert of sound, passion and music. Years of discomfort on the hard seats of the Christian Methodist Church in Arkansas had given me the talent to appear attentive while my real thoughts were focused in the distance.

What was I going to do with the money? Would I pay off the car or Guy's tuition or buy gold? I decided that if the university had displayed such patience so far, it could wait a little longer for Guy's tuition and my car payment, and I would have a gold necklace. I would have a necklace made of gold the color of sunrise and it would make my brown skin voluptuous, and I would at last buy a small piece of Kente cloth, red, gold and blue. I would ask the seamstress to make me a skirt so tight that it would mould my behind into a single roundness, and I would have to take mincing and coquettish steps.

Nana's sermon on the saintliness of Motherhood was falling, the tempo had slowed, Kwesi's encouragements had ceased. When Nana stopped talking there was a moment of respectful quiet.

I said, "Nana, I appreciate hearing that Africans cherish their mothers. It confirms my belief that in America we have retained more Africanisms than we know. For also among Black Americans Motherhood is sacred. We have strong mothers and we love them dearly."

Kwesi put his glass down. "Sister, I do not wish to contradict you, but isn't it true that the most common curse word among Americans imputes that the offender is the offspring of a female dog?"

What would he have said had he wanted to contradict me?

I said, "Brother, I was speaking not of Americans but Black Americans. We're not the same; we're more like you, if you haven't noticed."

Nana laughed, "She's got you, Kwesi." Kwesi kept his diplomatic smile and plunged directly to my heart.

"But, Sister, isn't it true that Black Americans and Black Americans alone, of all the people in the world, created a curse word which suggests that the accursed has known his own mother? Known her, that is, in a biblical sense?"

My rapier brain parried, "Yeah, yes, well, not really. I mean, I don't know.... Possibly in some other language ..." I was falling and Nana became my net. He said, "Kwesi, you know that the oppressed person, if convinced that he is worthless, looks to strike the person dearest to him. Oscar Wilde reminded us that we always hurt the thing we love. So it is human all over the world." He laughed, "Even in Harlem. Maybe especially Harlem. That is why we must do something special for our people in the diaspora. You in America have labored long and done well. Look at your schools, Fisk, Tuskegee, Atlanta University. You were slaves and now you head universities. Horace Mann Bond and St. Clair Drake are friends of mine." I had been ready to leave. After Kwesi spoke of the vulgarity heard so frequently in our neighborhoods, I was prepared to disappear in shame, but the mention of our schools and scholars was redemptive.

I smiled, "Oh yes, not all Blacks hate themselves."

Nana said, "We are well aware of that" (He often used the royal "we") "and now ... I asked you here to see if you are interested in a job in Kaneshie."

So I wasn't being offered a raise. All that daydreaming about gold had been a waste of time.

I said, "Kaneshie? That sounds lovely." It was horrible. Kaneshie was a bush town, 150 miles from Accra.

I continued, "But I am quite happy at Legon, and I think I am of use there. Kaneshie? They say it's beautiful country up there, but—"

Nana interrupted, "This job pays double your present salary and you will be provided with a bungalow and a new car."

Kwesi said, "Now that's looking after our people in the diaspora."

A move was not necessarily a negative thing. A house of my own in the heavily wooded area up north could be quite inviting, and with a new car I could drive to Accra in a few hours, and I could still buy that red-gold necklace and even a full kente cloth.

Kingdoms may fall and love may leave, but a dogged survival instinct is loyal to the end. I had never been promised nor (despite my secret hopes) did I expect certainty. I knew that God was in His heaven and anything might happen to His world. Kaneshie was the center of the diamond industry, and as I thought about it, it began to increase in promise. Rumors had it that people walking around might stumble upon diamonds laying in the road. I had not been a particularly lucky person, but just possibly I would find a lovely diamond to go with my gold necklace.

I said, "Nana, the idea interests me. What would be my duties?"

He answered, "You would do much as you are currently doing. Run the office. You can type of course?" He didn't wait so I didn't have time to lie. "And, I suppose, familiarize yourself with the working of a mine. Know the laborers, the output, the World Bank prices. This sort of thing. I'm sure you could do that."

I had always liked the idea of being someone's girl Friday. It promised responsibility with good pay and was a sort of marriage without sex.

"I'd be pleased to give it a try, and thanks to the person who mentioned me for the job."

Kwesi looked at me and wagged his head forward, then smiled and said, "Nana, I believe we have had a most fruitful meeting. Maya will do well in Kaneshie. It might be a little lonely at first, but your people will be coming up to see you and you will make friends. Now, Sister, do tell me how did you come to read my poetry?"

Nana said, "Kwesi, one minute. Poets are worse than prime ministers, always looking for ears. Maya, I'm going to send for my children. They should meet you."

Kwesi laughed, "Of course. The Budu-Arthur tribe. They are wonderful, and they are many."

Nana lifted his voice and hurled it into the universe.

"Children, come. Araba, Adae, Abenaa, Abaa, Ekua and Kwesi Budu-Arthur. Come, come and greet your American Auntie."

The clarion voice, enunciating the names with such force, prepared me for a schoolroom of children arriving in martial drill. Instead, a tall, slim, beautiful girl of fifteen entered the lighted area.

"Poppa, you wanted me?" Her voice lovely and musical.

Nana said, "Araba, yes, I want you and the others. Miss Angelou, this is my oldest child. Araba Budu-Arthur, Miss Angelou."

As he spoke, more children drifted in, talking among themselves. When five of them had gathered, Nana looked up and asked, "And Adae? As usual I must ask. And Adae?"

Four young voices answered him, but no meaning could be extracted from the din. When the noise reached a peak, another girl entered to stand with her siblings. Adae was nearly as tall as Araba, but while her older sister displayed a solemn dignity, Adae seemed to move even standing still. The children stood together like an often rehearsed theatrical troupe, their eyes focused on me.

I said, "I'm pleased to meet you all." Adae turned to

her siblings and said knowingly, "That's the way American Negroes speak. They say 'you all.'" She faced me again, while her brothers and small sisters examined me with obvious curiosity.

Adae said, "I'm pleased to meet you, Maya. Very pleased."

Keeping my voice low, I said, "As you have noticed, I am an American Negro, and among my people children do not call their elders by their first names. A fifteen-year-old girl [Adae was 15] would call me Mrs. Angelou, or if she liked me and I agreed she would address me as Auntie Maya. I will accept either." Adae looked at her older sister then at the young children. She looked at me for a very long minute.

"Very well, I don't know you yet, but I'll probably like you, so we will call you Auntie Maya. Do you agree?" She left me no time to respond. She nodded and said, "Good-bye, Auntie Maya. Good-bye, everybody." The four smaller children, as if on a signal, chorused, "Hello and good-bye, Auntie. Good-bye, everybody," and running, followed Adae from the room.

Nana, who had been silent during the exchange, spoke to Araba who was standing calmly before me. "And you, Araba, do you have something clever to say to Auntie Maya?" Her voice was as smooth as cream, and her smile was gentle. "Auntie, Adae knows that African children behave as you described Black American children do. She was acting the way European kids act at our school. Please overlook her, she's really a very nice person." Araba excused herself with the grace of a kindly monarch taking leave of adoring subjects. Kwesi and Nana smiled at each other.

Kwesi said to me, "That is the Budu-Arthur brood.

There is no way to tell what they will become, but I'd wager Adae will be president of the world and Araba will be its queen."

Nana shook his head and laughed to himself proudly, "My children." Then he looked over at me, "I do hope Adae didn't annoy you. It is through the eyes of strangers that a parent can see their children as people."

I denied any annoyance and said I'd like to see the children alone.

He agreed, then ordered the driver in one shout and modulated to continue speaking to me. "You will hear from me when an appointment is arranged." He offered me his hand, and I was tempted to kiss it, but checked myself just in time. I grasped his hand and shook it firmly.

"Thank you, Nana."

"Don't thank me, but when you go to Kaneshie let them know that your heart and head are concentrated on Africa and not, like most Americans, on Coca Cola and Cadillacs." Nana added, "And Maya, take your C.V."

The driver had come in. I asked, "C.V.?"

He said, "Curriculum vitae. Your schools, degrees and work history. Good night. Kwesi will see you to the car."

Kwesi was at my side being solicitous, the driver was standing beside the car, and I was laughing weakly. Kwesi noticed me trembling when he embraced me and probably credited my nervous response to meeting the great man.

"Sister, we must talk. You must come to me and my wife Molly. We will feed you and definitely no fish. Ha, ha."

If everyone knew my dietary restrictions, why didn't Nana know that I had not been to college? I should have said so on the spot. During the drive home, I berated myself for the show of cowardice. Obviously the temptation of a good job, large salary and European-style benefits were enough to send my much vaunted morality scurrying. It wasn't pleasant to admit that I was no more moral than the commercial bandits upon whom I heaped every crime from slavery to Hiroshima.

As soon as I reached my house, I decided that when Nana telephoned I would tell him to offer the job to Alice or Vicki. Then I pillowed myself in goodness and slept righteously.

When our grinning faces appeared at Julian's door, he tried waving his arms to distract us, but only succeeded in agitating the tell-tale odors of sage, oregano and fried pork. He had received another package of sausage from Washington, D.C. The Revolutionist Returnees had gotten wind of its arrival and converged on the Mayfield home in private cars, taxis and on foot. Julian, who was no more or less generous than the next person, put on a gruff face and said he was working and we had to leave, but when he saw we wouldn't be run off, he gave in and laughed. "Which one of you nuts was spying on the airport?"

Ana Livia brought a platter of sausage patties to the

porch, and we fell upon it with a savor unrelated to hunger. Homesickness was never mentioned in our crowd. Who would dare admit a longing for a White nation so full of hate that it drove its citizens of color to madness, to death or to exile? How to confess even to one's ownself, that our eyes, historically customed to granite buildings, wide paved avenues, chromed cars, and brown, black, beige, pink and white-skinned people, often ached for those familiar sights?

We chewed the well spiced pork of America, but in fact, we were ravenously devouring Houston and Macon, Little Rock and St. Louis. Our faces eased with sweet delight as we swallowed Harlem and Chicago's south side.

"All we need now is a plate of grits." That from Lesley Lacy who had probably never eaten grits in his life.

Julian brought out a bundle of week-old dailies from the States and dealt parcels out to us as if they were large floppy cards. He saved a magazine and held it above his head. "Here's my article on Baldwin in *Freedomways.*"

*Nobody Knows My Name,* James Baldwin's book, had passed through so many hands its pages were as fluffy as Kleenex and had caused fierce arguments. Some detractors denounced Baldwin as a creation of White America, adding that he had been constructed by the establishment for the establishment. His supporters argued that if White America had been smart enough to make a James Baldwin, obviously there would have been no need to create one. In New York City, Sylvester Leaks had disappointed some of his fans by attacking Baldwin. We in Ghana knew that Julian had written an article in support of the controversial author.

Julian, in his most roguish tone, said, "I'll put the magazine here. No tearing, scratching or biting, first come and all that shit." Alice moved like a whip, snatched up the magazine, which meant that she would take it home and that Vicki or I would be next in command.

Ana Livia spoke and took our total attention by announcing, "Dr. Du Bois is sick. Lucid, but very sick. He said he has stopped learning and it is time for him to go." Our small crowd made a large noise of protest. Du Bois was ninety-six years old, and frail, but we wanted him to live forever. He had no right to his desire for death. We argued that great men and women should be forced to live as long as possible. The reverence they enjoyed was a life sentence, which they could neither revoke nor modify.

When the discussion reached a noise level that prohibited all understanding, Julian said he had read about a march to Washington, D.C., to be led by Martin Luther King, Jr. The news of Dr. Du Bois' deteriorating health was driven away by an immediate buzzing of sarcastic questions.

"King leading a march. Who is he going to pray to this time, the statue of Abe Lincoln?"

"Give us our freedom again, please suh."

"King has been in jail so much he's got a liking for those iron bars and jailhouse food."

The ridicule fitted our consciousness. We were brave revolutionaries, not pussyfooting nonviolent cowards. We scorned the idea of being spat upon, kicked, and then turning our cheeks for more abuse. Of course, none of us, save Julian, had even been close to bloody violence, and not one of us had spent an hour in jail for our political beliefs.

My policy was to keep quiet when Reverend King's name was mentioned. I didn't want to remind my radical friends of my association with the peacemaker. It was difficult, but I managed to dispose of the idea that my silence was a betrayal. After all, when I worked for him, I had been deluded into agreeing with Reverend King that love would cure America of its pathological illnesses, that indeed our struggle for equal rights would redeem the country's baleful history. But all the prayers, sit-ins, sacrifices, jail sentences, humiliation, insults and jibes had not borne out Reverend King's vision. When maddened White citizens and elected political leaders vowed to die before they would see segregation come to an end, I became more resolute in rejecting nonviolence and more adamant in denying Martin Luther King.

Someone made the suggestions that although we were radicals, as Black Americans we should support our people in the States and form a march sympathetic to the Washington march. As products of a picketing, protesting era, we unanimously and immediately agreed. Of course, we would march on the American Embassy with placards and some appropriate shouts. Julian would investigate Ghana's policy on marches and secure permits if needed. Lesley would inform the Ghanaian students at the university who might like to join. Each of us excitedly chose assignments, feeling ourselves back on familiar ground. When it came to action we were in the church where we had been baptized. We knew when to moan, when to shout and when to start speaking in tongues.

Since Dr. Du Bois was too old and ill to accompany us, Julian would ask Dr. Alphaeus Hunton. Dr. Hunton was co-director with Dr. Du Bois of the Encyclopedia Africana, and would represent the older, more sober, more thoughtful segment of the Black American residents. We also decided to do more than march. Hundreds of thousands were expected at the Washington gathering and

Mahalia Jackson was to sing and Dr. King would speak. Our community couldn't even count on one hundred people, so we decided to write a stinging protest declaration and form a committee which would present it to the American ambassador inside the embassy. Our arrangements were made and agreed upon, and we broke up our meeting, our heads filled with a new and exciting charge and our fingers still smelling of spicy pork sausage.

The Washington March was to begin at 7:00 A.M. on August 27. Because of the seven-hour time difference, we planned to begin our supportive march at midnight on the twenty-sixth in the park across from the embassy.

The crowd, much larger than any of us expected, stumbled around in the dark greeting and embracing. I heard American voices which were new to me, and saw Guy arrive laughing with a group of young Ghanaian friends. At eighteen, he had a long history of marches, having participated in political protests since he was fourteen.

Alice and her Rhodesian friend appeared carrying sticks which had oiled rags wrapped tightly at one end. They would be lighted as we began our vigil.

Farmers and junior high school teachers, Black Ameri-

cans on holiday in Accra, and some Peace Corps volun-
teers swelled the ranks. We had begun to wonder about
Julian, who was late. Those of us close to him knew that
was unusual, since he was always punctual in political
matters.

The general atmosphere was festive, with little bursts of
laughter exploding in the humid darkness. We had
lighted some fire sticks when Julian arrived. He called a
few of us away from the crowd.

"Dr. Du Bois is dead." His face in the flickering light
was grey-black and his voice was flat. "I don't think we
should inform everyone, but you all should know."

Alice, pragmatic and direct, said, "Well, what timing.
He had a full and useful life and I think we should tell
everybody. They'll feel more like marching."

We agreed and fanned out carrying the important news
to the congregation. Sound became muffled as if Dr. Du
Bois himself had appeared and ordered immediate quiet
from the group. Suddenly someone whose voice I didn't
recognize began singing, "Oh, oh, Freedom, oh, oh, Freedom, oh, oh, Freedom over me.

> And before I'll be a slave
> I'll be buried in my grave
> And go home to my God
> And be free."

There were a few mumbles of opposition in the crowd.
"This is a political demonstration. Why are they singing
that Ole' Time Religion stuff?"

The detractor was drowned out as voices joined the so-
loist. We were singing for Dr. Du Bois' spirit, for the inval-
uable contributions he made, for his shining intellect and
his courage. To many of us he was the first American

Negro intellectual. We knew about Jack Johnson and Jesse Owens and Joe Louis. We were proud of Louis Armstrong and Marian Anderson and Roland Hayes. We memorized the verses of James Weldon Johnson, Langston Hughes, Paul Laurence Dunbar and Countee Cullen, but they were athletes, musicians and poets, and White folks thought all those talents came naturally to Negroes. So, while we survived because of those contributors and their contributions, the powerful White world didn't stand in awe of them. Sadly, we also tended to take those brilliances for granted. But W.E.B. Du Bois and of course Paul Robeson were different, held on a higher or at least on a different plateau than the others.

We marched and sang thinking of home and the thousands who were marching in Washington, D.C., and many of us held in our minds a picture of the dapper little man, sporting a vandyke beard, perfectly groomed, who earned a Harvard doctorate before the end of the 1800's and who said in 1904, "The problem of the twentieth century will be the problem of the color line."

Dawn drifted in on a ragged file of damp and worn out marchers. During the early morning hours, a West African tropical downpour had drenched us and sent us scurrying to cars and trees and doorways. The African marchers said they could have forewarned us. They knew that a driving rain always followed the death of a great soul.

I asked, "God weeps?"

"Of course not. It is the way the spirits welcome a great soul to the land of the dead. They wash it first."

We had walked in the dark, through the flickering light of oil sticks, protesting American racism and extolling the indomitability of the human spirit.

But daylight brought a hard reality. We were in fact

marching against the American Embassy. It was a large impressive building made more impressive by the marines who lay belly down on its rooftop pointing shining guns in our direction.

Our lines had diminished through the night. People who had jobs or children or appointments or reservations had slipped away. Although there had been an agreement that we would march in relays, I was happy that none of the Revolutionist Returnees had left. Julian was still trudging along like Sisyphus on his unending climb. Bobby and Sarah Lee walked together chatting in the way of old marrieds, calm as if out for a morning stroll. Lesley and Jim Lacy remained, their faces still showing youthful anger. Vicki, Alice, Kofi Bailey, Guy, a few Black Americans I didn't know and some Ghanaians continued walking. Everyone stopped, as if on signal, when two soldiers came out of the embassy door carrying a folded American flag. They stepped smartly to the flag pole, ignoring us, and began the routine movements of raising the banner.

Someone in our group shouted, "This isn't Iwo Jima, guys." Another screamed, "You haven't taken Bunker Hill, you know. This is Africa."

The incident fed energy to our tired bodies and we began to laugh. One of the soldiers was Black and during the ceremony, no doubt nervous, the soldiers fumbled and the flag began to sag toward the ground. It was the Black man who hurriedly caught the cloth and folded it lovingly into the White soldier's arms.

Some of us jeered, "Why you, brother? What has that flag done for you?"

"Brother, why don't you come over here and join us?"

"That flag won't cover you in Alabama."

The soldiers finished attaching the flag and began

drawing the ropes. As the flag ascended, our jeering increased. A careful listener could have heard new vehemence of our shouts. We were scorning the symbol of hypocrisy and hope. Many of us had only begun to realize in Africa that the Stars and Stripes was our flag and our only flag, and that knowledge was almost too painful to bear. We could physically return to Africa, find jobs, learn languages, even marry and remain on African soil all our lives, but we were born in the United States and it was the United States which had rejected, enslaved, exploited, then denied us. It was the United States which held the graves of our grandmothers and grandfathers. It was in the United States, under conditions too bizarre to detail, that those same ancestors had worked and dreamed of "a better day, by and by." There we had learned to live on the head of burnt matches, and sleep in holes in the ground. In Arkansas and Kansas and Chattanooga, Tennessee, we had decided to be no man's creature. In Dallas we put our shoulders to the wheel, and our hands in God's hand in Tulsa. We had learned the power of power in Chicago, and met in Detroit insatiable greed. We had our first loves in the corn brakes of Mississippi, in the cotton fields of Georgia we experienced the thundering pleasure of sex, and on 125th Street and 7th Avenue in Harlem the Holy Spirit called us to be His own.

I shuddered to think that while we wanted that flag dragged into the mud and sullied beyond repair, we also wanted it pristine, its white stripes, summer cloud white. Watching it wave in the breeze of a distance made us nearly choke with emotion. It lifted us up with its promise and broke our hearts with its denial.

We hurled invectives against the soldiers' retreating backs, knowing that the two young men were not our ene-

mies and that our sneers did not hide our longing for full
citizenship under that now undulating flag.

In the early afternoon, Julian, Alice, Jean Pierre, Dr.
Hunton and I walked past the nervous eyes of guards and
into the embassy. The calm first secretary, standing in for
the absent ambassador, accepted our written protest and
told us he would see that it got into the hands of the
proper authorities. He smiled and said a chummy, "My
wife is marching in Washington with Reverend King. I
wish I could be there."

The ceremony was unsatisfactory. We joined the once
again large crowd of marchers and explained what we had
done, and the march was over.

I went home alone, emptied of passion and too exhausted to cry.

Malcolm had arrived at midday in Accra, and by evening
the Mayfields' house was filled with expatriates eager to
meet and listen to him. We sat on chairs, stools, tables and
hunched on the floor, excited into a trembling silence.

"I am still a Muslim. I am still a minister and I am still
Black." The golden man laughed, and lamplight entan-
gled itself in his sandy beard.

"My trip to Mecca has changed many other things

about me. That is what the Hadj is supposed to do, and when I return to America I will make some statements which will shock everybody." He rubbed his beard and his eyes were quick with humor. "Of course, I suppose people would be really shocked, if Malcolm X wasn't shocking."

The crowd responded in quick unison like a laugh track for a television comedy. Those who knew him were surprised at Malcolm's light-heartedness.

When I met him two years earlier, he had been the bombastic spokesman for Elijah Muhammad's Nation of Islam. Clean shaven and dark-suited, he sizzled proudly on street corners and from television screens, as he called Whites "Blue-eyed devils" and accused America of totalitarian genocide.

Just as Jomo Kenyatta was Kenya's "Burning Spear," so Malcolm X was America's Molotov cocktail, thrown upon the White hope that all Black Americans would follow the nonviolent tenets of Dr. Martin Luther King. "Freedom at any cost" had been his rallying cry. He had been the stalking horse for the timid who openly denied him but took him, like a forbidden god, into their most secret hearts, there to adore him.

The living room and side porch were filled with an attentive and shocked audience, as Malcolm, still at ease, sat describing his recent pilgrimage to Mecca.

"Brothers and Sisters, I am pleased to see you all here in the homeland and bring you news which won't come as news to you from that place you left. The situation has not lightened up. Black people are still marching, sitting in, praying in and even swimming in."

We all knew that the Muslims had shown disgust with the Black American integrationists.

He continued, "And White Americans are still saying

that they don't want Blacks in their restaurants, churches, swimming pools and voting booths. I thought I'd bring you familiar news first. Now this is new news." Those of us on the floor and those who had found chairs leaned eagerly toward Malcolm.

"I have had to rethink a number of things." He said that though his basic premise that the United States was a racist country held true, he no longer believed that all Whites were devils, nor that any human being was inherently cruel at birth. "On this journey to Mecca, I met White men with blue eyes, who I can call brother with conviction. That means that I am forced to reconsider statements I have made in the past and I must have the courage to speak up and out about those reconsiderations."

His possession of language had not diminished, nor had his magnetic aura lessened. We sat enthralled at what he said and how he said it.

"I am not in favor among the followers of the Honorable Elijah Muhammad, and this new statement will anger them more, but our people are in need of truth and I have tried and will continue to try to speak only truth to the people. The teaching of the Honorable Elijah Muhammad enabled me to break the noose that ignorance and racism put around my neck, and I will always thank Allah and the Honorable Elijah Muhammad for that. But a person must make the effort to learn, and growing is the inevitable reward of learning."

He never mentioned the Islamic leader's name without the salutary designation, and although he was speaking to a very informal gathering in a homey living room, save for the lowered volume of his voice, he might well have been addressing an audience of thousands in Harlem.

Julian asked him to tell us why he came to Ghana.

Malcolm set his tea cup on a nearby table and, lacing his long fingers, began a sawing motion with them which was his only physical indication of tension.

After Mecca he had stopped in Cairo and met Egyptian government officials and David Du Bois, and had gone to Nigeria to confer with other African politicians. He needed as many governmental contacts as possible so that when he took the case of the Black American before the General Assembly of the United Nations, he could be sure at least of some African and maybe other nationals' support.

Every complexion of political persuasion was present in Julian's house that evening. There were true revolutionaries, counter-revolutionaries, petit bourgeois, capitalists, communists, hedonists, socialists, humanitarians and aging beatniks. When Malcolm mentioned arguing for our people before the United Nations, we shouted spontaneously and with one voice of approval. He said, "If our cause was debated by all the world's nations, it would mean that finally, we would be taken seriously. We could stop courting the 'fair-minded white people in the U.S.' as Martin Luther King called some of his constituents. America would be forced to face up to its discriminatory policies. Street protests and sit-ins would be as passé as auction blocks and as unnecessary as manumission papers. If South African Blacks can petition the U.N. against their country's policy of apartheid, then America should be shown on the world's stage as a repressionist and bestial racist nation."

A single question arose from that diverse group, and Alice put it into words. "Do you want us to arrange for you to meet Ghanaian officials and to see President Nkrumah?"

The serious scowl left Malcolm's brow. He looked

around at the company, spending a few seconds on each face. Then he smiled.

"Black Americans! You all are really something." He laughed aloud. "You people just got here and already you know the President."

His laughter rang high, giving us license to join him and forget that of the forty or so people gathered, only Julian had actually met President Nkrumah and, although we all sported posters and drawings of the handsome leader, most of us had never even seen him in the flesh.

In the now relaxed atmosphere, Malcolm furnished us stories of his journey. Some were just funny and others were funny and bitter.

"I was waiting at the Nigerian Airport when a White man came up and spoke to me. He offered his hand so I shook it. Then he grinned and said, 'I've admired you, Mr. X, truly admired you.' I asked him, 'Would you have shaken my hand in New York?' He went red as a fire engine and said, 'I don't suppose so.' So I asked why he felt it was all right to do so in Africa, and that man had the nerve to get indignant. He said, 'Well, we're both Americans!' "

Our merry response was totally lacking in merriment. We laughed, as usual, because of the truth in the incident and because there was nothing else to do about it.

When Malcolm followed Ana Livia to the buffet dinner in the dining room, a few people sat pooling knowledge like children gathering pennies to buy a special treat.

"How well do you know Kofi Batcha?"

"And surely . . . , the Minister of Defense can be approached."

"I think he owes me one."

"If you can't be sure, he certainly won't remember."

"He should meet Nana Nketsia."

"T. D. Bafoo will be of help."

"Efua Sutherland can open some doors."

"How about Geoffrey Bing?"

"He's White, old, out of favor, and going senile."

"But he knows where the bodies will be buried and who will dance on whose grave."

"What about Michael Dei-Anan?" We agreed to contact the poet-statesman who always had an available ear for a Black American.

In one week we were able to introduce Malcolm to Ghanaian Cabinet Ministers, the African and European Diplomatic Corps as well as the Cuban and Chinese ambassadors. Julian, Ana Livia, Lesley and I were his chauffeurs, while Vicki was secretary.

The Ghana Press Club gave a party in Malcolm's honor, a mighty unusual action for that band of journalists. We arrived to warm handshakes, drum rolls, shouts of praise and music from the open air dance floor. Malcolm accepted the greetings with appreciation and then sat at a table and absorbed himself in the people dancing nearby. I thought he was enjoying the spectacle of pretty women and suave men moving sensually to the rhythms of the

High Life, West Africa's most popular dance, but I noticed his hands were in his lap and he was lacing his fingers, first this way, then the other, then this way, then. . . .

When the High Life Orchestra took its break, a Ghanaian journalist asked Malcolm to speak. He neither rushed nor lagged through the festive party air, but at the microphone, under the stars, Malcolm began soberly.

"First, Brothers and Sisters, thank you for inviting me to the Ghana Press Club. I do not want you to think that because I have been sitting quietly, that I do not appreciate your invitation. The fact is, I am in no mood to dance. I think of our brothers and sisters at home, squirming under the heel of racial oppression, and I do not care to dance. I think of our brothers and sisters in the Congo, squirming under the heel of imperialist invasion, and I do not care to dance. I think of our brothers and sisters in Southern Africa squirming under the heel of apartheid, and I do not care to dance."

The crowd was not pleased to have their gaiety censored, and a few disapproving murmurs could be heard. They were drowned out by the strong voices of T. D. Bafoo, Kofi Batcha, Cameron Duodu and Nurru Bello Damz who were standing at their respective tables.

"Hear! Hear! Hear, Hear!" And "Speak! Speak!"

Fortunately, Malcolm's speech was brief, and when the orchestra returned the celebrants crowded again onto the floor, dancing, flirting, wiggling and inviting. Obviously they sympathized with the African struggle everywhere, naturally they supported the aspirations for freedom, but their country was in their own hands. President Nkrumah was the "Mass pass Mass," the person who surpassed others, and their revolution was a success.

"Ye. Ye." The time had come to dance.

Alice looked at Malcolm, then wagged her head at me, and I thought of my grandmother who said, "If you want to know how important you are to the world, stick your finger in a pond and pull it out. Will the hole remain?"

When Malcolm met Nana Nketsia the two men acted magnetized. I had not heard Nana speak so quietly nor seen Malcolm listen so deeply. Each man grew in the other's presence and when I took Malcolm to his hotel, he said, "Now I have met African royalty. A chief. True, true. He knows his people and he loves them, and they love him." Malcolm's face wore a mask of wistfulness so telling I had to look away.

Lesley arranged for him to speak at Legon University, and that night the auditorium was filled with students, lecturers and some townsfolk. Since Malcolm was the guest of the young Marxist League, the organization's representative spoke first. The young man quoted Karl Marx with such force, he seemed to have taken on his subject's persona. The crowd became impatient, but Malcolm sat on the stage calmly listening to the speaker.

Guy had given me the honor of agreeing to sit near me. He and his Ghanaian friends were equally anxious for the Marxist to leave the podium so that Malcolm could speak, and they began to murmur. I coughed to get Guy's attention, but he looked at me and frowned. His scowl said, "Don't reprimand me in public. Don't embarrass me." He was right. He was nineteen and each of us had labored with some success to create new ways to talk to each other. Nature was guiding his hands to loosen the maternal bonds, and although I felt if I was freed from the stay of motherhood, I might fly away like a feather in the wind, with trepidation, I too tried to let my child become his own man.

Finally, Lesley Lacy introduced Malcolm and immediately his oratorical skill captured the audience. The years in prison, in mosques, on street corners, at college lecterns and before television cameras had produced a charismatic speaker who could play an audience as great musicians play instruments. He spoke moderately loud, then thundered, whispered, then roared. He used the imagery of Black American Baptist preachers and the logic of university intellectuals. He spoke of America, White and Black Americans, racism, hate and the awful need to be treated as humans.

When he finished the audience rose. A group of students which included Guy, began to chant the football cheer, "Asante Kotoko."

Malcolm quieted the crowd and asked for questions.

He met each question squarely. The audience applauded. A faculty member asked why Malcolm incited people to violence. Why did he preach violence? He answered, "I am responding to violence. If your house is on fire and I come to warn you, why should you accuse me of setting the fire? You should thank me for my concern. Maybe you can put out the fire before it is too late."

The Africans relished Malcolm's use of proverbs. His

answers were as considered and detailed as his address had been. Then a student stood, "Mr. Malcolm X, what I don't understand is why you call yourself Black. You look more like a White man than a Negro." The young man sat down and a few embarrassed titters and some disapproving groans could be heard on the dark floor.

At first Malcolm laughed. He opened his mouth wide and laughed loud and long.

"Little brother, I've been waiting for that question since I landed in Africa, and while many people thought it, you're the first person who had the nerve to ask. I commend your courage. Well, let's look at it. At home, that is, in that place where I was born, I've been called by Whites a yellow nigger, a light-skinned nigger, a red uppity nigger, a fair-skinned seditious nigger, but never until now have I been called a White man. I mean, Whites who should know their own have never made the mistake of overlooking my African blood. It is a strange sensation to have to explain, in Africa, the effects of slavery, and maybe the young man who asked the question is the only person who really needs an explanation, but if there are others, I suggest that you all listen carefully.

"As slaves, we were the property of slave masters. Our men were worked to death, our women were raped, then worked to death, and many of our children were born looking like me. The slave master fathers denied their children, but fortunately we retained enough Africanisms to believe that the mother's child was our child, no matter who or what the father had been.

"Before I became a Muslim, when I was hustling on the streets of America, because of my color, Black people called me mariney, and Detroit Red. Some even cussed me out and called me unprintable names, but nobody tried to give me away to White folks. I was accepted. Now, my point is, if Whites who should know don't claim me, and Blacks who should know do claim me, I think it's clear where I belong. I am a Black man. Notice, I don't say Black American, I don't consider myself a democrat, a republican, or an American. I am a Black Muslim man of African heritage. Next?"

Black Americans led the applause and soon the entire audience was standing, clapping and laughing its approval.

Malcolm's time was perforated in orderly sections like postage stamps. He went to see Lesley at Legon, visited with Sarah and Bobby Lee in their home, called upon Alphaeus and Dorothy Hunton and still had energy many evenings to fill Julian's living room with a fluency of strong language and his always unexpected humor.

We congratulated ourselves on our successes, but commiserated over our largest failure. Despite all our efforts we were not able to get Malcolm an audience with Kwame Nkrumah.

Some thought that the President's reluctance to meet the radical Black leader stemmed from a desire to stay in America's good graces. That idea was argued down since Nkrumah's policies tended decidedly toward nonalignment. There were as many Russians in Ghana as Americans, and they seemed to be treated equally.

Julian tried to reach Shirley Graham Du Bois, but she was not available. Mrs. Du Bois could have arranged a meeting in seconds. She and the president were family-close. It was said that Nkrumah called her "little mother," and that she telephoned him each night at bedtime. Ana Livia, the late Doctor Du Bois' doctor, telephoned her and even went to the Du Bois home, but Shirley was as elusive as smoke in a high wind. I accused her of being deliberately inaccessible, but after my friends said that my paranoia had gotten out of hand again, I kept my thoughts to myself.

The Nigerian High Commissioner, Alhadji Isa Wali, invited Malcolm to lunch and a few of us tagged along. We sat in the Residency dining room, watching our leader work a subtle charm on the already enchanted diplomat.

It was clear that Malcolm had a number of integrated personae. None was contradictory to the others, but each was different. When he sat with me after a long day of interviews and meetings, he was a big brother advisor, suggesting that it was time for me to come home. "The country needs you. Our people need you. Alice and Julian and Max Bond and Sylvia, you should all come home. You have seen Africa, bring it home and teach our people about the homeland." He talked of his family. "Betty is the sweetest woman in the world, and the girls. Did I show you these pictures?" Each time I would deny that I had seen the photographs and each time he would point out and name his daughters.

In the late evenings, he was like a traveling salesman or a soldier on duty, a family man, sadly away from those he loved most.

But in the larger formal company of Black American expatriates, he told humorous stories about Whites and about himself. He entertained easily and was quick to laugh.

On stages, he spoke fiercely against oppression and for revolution. "I am neither a fanatic nor a dreamer. I am a Black man who loves justice and loves his people."

And with the Nigerian High Commissioner, who at five feet stood fourteen inches shorter than Malcolm, he was a large attentive son, explaining himself endearingly to his small father.

"We have much work to do at home. Even as you have your work here in Africa. We are lambs in a den of wolves. We will need your help. Only with the help of Africa and Africans can we succeed in freeing ourselves." His voice was soft, his volume low, still he spoke with force.

After lunch we gathered on the veranda so that Alice could take her photographs for history. The ambassador presented Malcolm with a grand bou bou, which he quickly put on. The rich robe which had fallen to the floor when worn by High Commissioner Alhadji Isa Wali came just below Malcolm's knees. Both men laughed at the difference in size, but the ambassador said, "Some are big, some are small, but we are all one."

The Chinese Residency was festive with lights and music on Malcolm's last night in Ghana and our jollity matched the atmosphere. Vicki was being courted by the Chinese delegation. They offered her a trip to China and an opportunity to stay there and teach. Alice had applied for a job with the E.C.A., based in Addis Ababa, and her chances looked good.

We wore our prettiest dresses and best smiles and when

we entered the large salon our hosts greeted us as if they had hardly been able to await our arrival. (After a few minutes I noticed that they greeted each new guest as generously.) Julian and Ana Livia were already there with Malcolm mingling in the crowded room. Drinks were brought on large trays and a pretty variety of foods waited on buffets.

The Cuban ambassador and his glamorous wife were talking earnestly with Malcolm when Shirley Du Bois entered. She was a medium-sized, light brown-skinned woman with large eyes, a long attractive face and the confidence of Mount Kilimanjaro. After being welcomed by those in her path, she walked immediately to Malcolm and, taking him by the arm, guided him to a corner where they sat.

The guests swirled around each other, exchanging conversational partners as if they were participants in a jamboree. After nearly an hour, Shirley and Malcolm emerged from their retreat and rejoined the party.

Shirley said loudly, "This man is brilliant. I am taking him for my son. He must meet Kwame. They have too much in common not to meet." On that decisive statement she took her leave. Malcolm spent a few more minutes talking with our hosts, then Julian said since Malcolm was to travel the next morning he would drive him to the Continental Hotel.

I was in a rage when I drove my housemates home.

"Are you ready for Shirley Du Bois? 'I'm taking him for my son.' Hell, before she wouldn't even see him. I can't stand that." Alice and Vicki let me rant alone. I didn't mind that they acted indifferent to Shirley's belated acceptance of Malcolm, I was enjoying my anger.

We were ready for bed when the telephone rang. Alice

answered it, while Vicki and I stood by nervously. No one in Accra telephoned after eleven o'clock, save to announce a crisis.

Alice hung up the phone and turned to us. She was somewhere between laughing and crying.

"Kwame Nkrumah will see Malcolm at nine o'clock in the morning. Julian is taking him to Flagstaff House."

Vicki whooped and hollered, "Success! Success!" She grabbed me, then Alice, then me again. Alice was a little stunned and I was furious.

I said, "Shirley went straight home and called the President and told him he had to see Malcolm. She could have done that a week ago, but no."

Alice agreed, but Vicki said, "Better late than never. You all ought to be celebrating, I say."

For me sleep was difficult that night. My bed was lumpy with anger and my pillow a rock of intemperate umbrage.

The next morning we met Malcolm after his visit with President Nkrumah. The bright sunshine, the bougainvillaea and the singing birds around the hotel didn't brighten my countenance. I claimed to be saddened by Malcolm's pending departure, but in fact my heart was still hardened to Shirley Du Bois. Rather than inquire about the Nkrumah interview, I stood apart pouting, while Alice snapped photos and Julian put Malcolm's luggage in the car. A convoy of limousines glided up importantly to the hotel's porte-cochere. Small flags waved from the hoods of luxury cars, which meant that each car carried an ambassador.

Alice said there must be some diplomatic meeting, and began to pose Malcolm and Julian for a picture. As she finished, the Nigerian High Commissioner approached.

"My people, good morning. Brother Malcolm, morning. A few of us have come to accompany you to the airport." The gesture was so unexpected that even Malcolm was speechless.

The Nigerian diplomat continued, "The Chinese, Guinea, Yugoslav, Mali, Cuban, Algerian and Egyptian ambassadors are here. Others wanted to come but national matters detained them. We will pull up and onto the road as you will want to ride with your friends. We will follow."

Julian was the first to speak to Malcolm after the High Commissioner left us.

"Man, we ought to pay you for this visit. You've given this poor group of Black exiles some status. Forty-five minutes with the president and now a convoy of limousines to see you to the airport. Man! We were living here before, but after your visit we have really arrived."

We were all laughing with pleasure when we heard the familiar sounds of Black American speech. We turned around and saw Muhammad Ali coming out of the hotel with a large retinue of Black men. They were all talking and joking among themselves. One minute after we saw them, they saw Malcolm.

The moment froze, as if caught on a daguerreotype, and the next minutes moved as a slow montage. Muhammad stopped, then turned and spoke to a companion. His friends looked at him. Then they looked back at Malcolm. Malcolm also stopped, but he didn't speak to us, nor did any of us have the presence of mind to say anything to him. Malcolm had told us that after he severed ties to the Nation of Islam, many of his former friends had become hostile.

Muhammad and his group were the first to turn away.

They started walking toward a row of parked cars. Malcolm, with a rush, left us and headed toward the departing men. We followed Malcolm. He shouted, "Brother Muhammad. Brother Muhammad."

Muhammad and his companions stopped and turned to face Malcolm.

"Brother, I still love you, and you are still the greatest." Malcolm smiled a sad little smile. Muhammad looked hard at Malcolm, and shook his head.

"You left the Honorable Elijah Muhammad. That was the wrong thing to do, Brother Malcolm." His face and voice were also sad. Malcolm had been his supporter and hero. Disappointment and hurt lay on Muhammad's face like dust. Abruptly, he turned and walked away. His coterie followed. After a few steps they began talking again, loudly.

Malcolm's shoulders sagged and his face was suddenly gloomy. "I've lost a lot. A lot. Almost too much." He led us back to my car. "I want to ride with Maya and Julian. We'll meet at the airport." Alice and the other friends rode with Ana Livia and three six-footers tried to be comfortable in my little Fiat. Even when we saw the diplomat's limousines following us, the heavy mood seemed destined to stay.

Malcolm broke the silence. "Now, Sister, what do you think of Shirley Du Bois?" The question gave me a chance to articulate my anger, and I let loose. I spoke of her lack of faith, her lack of identity with Black American struggle, her isolation from her people, her pride at sitting in the catbird seat in Ghana. Malcolm let me continue until my tirade wound down.

"Now, Sister, I thought you were smart, but I see you are very childish, dangerously immature." He had not spoken so harshly before to anyone in Ghana—I was shocked.

"Have you considered that her husband has only been dead a few months? Have you considered that at her age she needs some time to consider that she is walking around wounded, limping for the first time in many years on one leg?"

Tears were bathing my face, not for the sad picture Malcolm was drawing of Shirley, but for myself as the object of his displeasure.

Julian, from his uncomfortable seat in the back of the car, put his hand on my shoulder gently, "Keep your eyes on the road."

Malcolm said, "Sister, listen and listen carefully. Picture American racism as a mountain. Now slice that mountain from the top to the bottom and open it like a door. Do you see all the lines, the strata?" I could hardly see the road ahead, but I nodded.

"Those are the strata of American life and we are being attacked on each one. We need people on each level to fight our battle. Don't be in such a hurry to condemn a person because he doesn't do what you do, or think as you think or as fast. There was a time when you didn't know what you know today." His voice had become more explanatory and less accusatory.

"When you hear that the Urban League or the NAACP is giving a formal banquet at the Waldorf-Astoria, I know you won't go, but don't knock them. They give scholarships to poor Black children. One of those recipients might become a Julian Mayfield, or a Maya Angelou, or a Malcolm X. You understand?"

I would have died rather than say I disagreed. I said, "I will think about that."

He said, "I can't ask anymore. I admire all of you. Our people can be proud. Julian will tell you about my meeting with Nkrumah. I wanted to ride with you to encourage you to broaden your thinking. You are too good a woman to think small. You know we, I mean in the United States and elsewhere, are in need of hard thinkers. Serious thinkers, who are not timid. We are called upon to defend ourselves all the time. In every arena." Malcolm had lost his harshness and seemed to be reflecting rather than addressing either me or Julian.

Julian asked him if Muhammad's actions at the hotel came as a surprise, and Malcolm did not answer directly. "He is young. The Honorable Elijah Muhammad is his prophet and his father, I understand. Be kind to him for his sake, and mine. He has a place in my heart."

At the airport, the ambassadors and other well-wishers swooped him away. Alice had time to arrange him for one last photo and we all shook his hand and hugged him.

Julian said in a forbidding tone, "Man, I don't like to see you traveling alone. You know there's a price on your head."

Malcolm smiled. "No one can guard anyone's life. Not even his own. Only Allah can protect. And he has let me slide so far." He smiled for us all and then was gone.

The letdown affected our speech. There seemed to be no words to describe what we were feeling. We regarded each other with embarrassment. Malcolm's presence had elevated us, but with his departure, we were what we had been before: a little group of Black folks, looking for a home.

I still found myself grinning when I came unexpectedly upon a clasp of confident Ghanaian children whispering in Ga or Fanti, their little legs shining and shimmering like oiled eels; my breath still crowded in my throat at the sight of African soldiers, chests thrust forward, stiffened legs and behinds high like peacocks' tails. The forests had lost none of their mystery and the bush villages were still enchanting. But Ghana was beginning to tug at me and make me uncomfortable, like an ill fitting coat.

The job at the diamond mine had been filled before I was obliged to test my morality or lie about my academic background. Nana had become a close and generous friend who continued seeking a better paying position for me, and I spent good times with his children and friends. I was welcome in many Ghanaian homes and had sufficient male company to satisfy my needs and vanity. My house-mates and the other Revolutionist Returnees provided opportunities for strong political debate and laughter, but I had to admit that I had begun to feel that I was not in my right place. Every moment in Ghana called attention to itself and each social affair was self-conscious. When I went dancing, between the beats and during the steps, I thought, "Here I am, Maya Angelou, dancing in Africa. I know I'm having a good time." Shopping in the crowded streets I thought, "This is me at last, really me, buying peppers in Makola market, aren't I lucky?" I decided that I was too aware of my location; not just in Accra, or in Adabraka, or Asylum Down.

I needed to get away from Africa and its cache of subtle promises and at least second-hand memories. I blamed the entire continent and history for my malaise when the real reason was more pointedly specific and as personal as a migraine.

Guy was troubling me. I was questioning my worth as a mother, and since I had been a parent over half my life, I thought if I failed in that role, success in any other area would have very little meaning.

One evening, a Ghanaian friend had come bringing gin and a terrible piece of gossip. He opened the fresh bottle, poured a few drops on the ground for the spirits, then we seated ourselves and drank comfortably.

"Sister, I have bad news about your son." My first thought was that he had been in another accident. As soon as that idea came it vanished; I would have been telephoned.

"What news, Brother?" I stayed seated in a fake serenity.

"It is said that he has a girlfriend."

I laughed, "Well, I hope so."

"Don't laugh, Sister. This certain friend is thirty-six years old and is an American and works for the American Embassy."

As I was asking, "What?" thoughts tumbled over themselves in my mind.

The woman was a year older than I. Couldn't she find any lover older than my nineteen-year-old son? An

American government employee? Ghanaians were still a little suspicious of all Americans, especially Black diplomats and employees in the embassy. I had just been made a member of the Ghana Press Club. Undoubtedly, suspicion would fall on me if the gossip was true.

"Brother, I thank you for the information. I will see to my son. Shall we freshen our drinks?"

I would not allow my informant to warn me that young men in love are like elephants in rutting time, difficult to dissuade. I knew that I could always talk to Guy.

The next day I took a break from a play in production after a student told me that my son was outside. Guy and I stood on the lawn in front of the National Theatre.

He appeared two inches taller than he had been the week before, and I had not noticed that he had grown a moustache.

"I am told that you have a girlfriend."

He had the nerve to be annoyed with me and, worse, to show his annoyance. "Mother, did you actually call me into town to talk about that?"

"I am told that she is thirty-six years old, and works for the American Embassy."

"Yes?" When a nineteen-year-old decides to clothe himself in dignity, nothing but pity or abject fear can penetrate his armor. I was too angry to ask for sympathy and obviously Guy had moved beyond fear of my disapproval.

"Is it true?"

"Oh, Mother, really. Don't you think it's time I had a life of my own?"

How could his life be separate from my life? I had been a mother of a child so long I had no preparation for life on any other level. As usual, anger, my enemy, betrayed me. I looked up at the young golden brown giant towering above my head.

"I will knock you down, Guy. Right here in front of God and everybody. Knock you down, do you hear?" I hadn't struck him since he was seven years old and had told me that I was too big to hit a small child.

"I will knock you down and I mean it."

His smile came from his new grown-up and distant place, and cut my heart to shreds.

He patted my head, "Yes, little mother. I'm sure you will." Then he turned and walked away.

When he closed up and left me no entry, a sense of loss rendered me momentarily unstable.

His existence had defined my own. As a child his sense of humor, attraction for puns and affection for me had lightened the single parent burden. He learned to read early because I loved to read, and I taught him to recite the poetry I had memorized in my own youth. When my seven-year-old son stood before me, beating the bones of his young chest, disclaiming, "It matters not how dark the night, how charged with punishments the scroll, I am the master of my fate, I am the captain of my soul," I saw myself, as if thrown upon a screen, clearly brave, clearly sure, sculpting a good life from resistant stone.

As my mother had done for me, I told him jokes and encouraged him to laugh at life and at himself. The Black child must learn early to allow laughter to fill his mouth or the million small cruelties he encounters will congeal and clog his throat.

Guy had been a good student, but did not develop into excellence because of our brief stays in cities where we lived. When he graduated from high school at the American College in Cairo, he told me he had gone to nineteen schools in eleven years. I was sorry to think that I hadn't noticed, but realized at the time I couldn't have changed our movements or destinations.

I had begun dancing or singing for a living when he was seven, and contracts took me from San Francisco to New York, and all the cities between the coasts. My family and even school administrators disapproved of what they thought was my vagabond life, but I was unable to live their ideals. I had no formal education, and no training other than in dance.

Once I was called to a Los Angeles school by the child psychologist. She was a White woman, in a white smock, in a white office.

"Miss Angelou, Guy is not doing well in school because he is hyperactive. I believe that comes from being moved around so frequently."

I sat still, looking at her, knowing that nothing she could say would influence the lives my son and I would lead.

She leaned back and pronounced, "He needs to stay put. He needs an established home life. I know that you are an entertainer and have to travel in your work, but maybe you could leave him with someone in your family. Your mother would look after him, perhaps?"

My mother, whom I loved dearly, had left me with my paternal grandmother from the time I was three until my thirteenth year. She had matured since then and become my reliable friend and a doting mother, but Guy was my responsibility and my joy.

I said nothing. The psychologist became uncomfortable as I sat silent. "He needs security, Miss Angelou. Stability will give him that security."

I stood and spoke. "Thank you for your concern and your time, Doctor, but I am his security. Wherever we go, we go together. Wherever he is he knows that that six-foot-tall Black woman is not too far away. What I don't furnish in stability, I make up in love. Good day."

We left a few weeks later for Chicago, another apartment hotel and another school.

His teens had not been easy for either of us. As he grew older, he began to withdraw, and because I didn't understand that an avalanche of sexuality had fallen upon him, I felt betrayed at his withdrawal. In our worst moments however, we had been saved by love and laughter.

But now, here in Ghana where neither of us was threatened by racial hate, where we both had separate and reasonably good lives, where it seemed we could both be happy, he had moved beyond my reach and into the arms of a cradle robber. Speaking to the woman would be a mistake. If she agreed to end the relationship, Guy would hate me for taking away his play pretty, and if she refused, we would have a fist fight.

I needed to get away from him and myself and the situation. Maybe to Europe, or Asia. I never thought of returning to America.

The cable from New York City shook the blues away. It read: "Berlin Volksopera wants original company Blacks, four days, stop. Venice Biennale, three days, stop. Ticket paid, plus salary. Can you come?" It was signed: Sidney Bernstein. Three years earlier, I had been a member of a cast which successfully presented Jean Genet's scathing play in New York City. At first, I gave little thought to either the play or the other actors. I was ecstatic with the thought of separating myself from Guy and his brand new grown-up ways.

I rushed to talk to Alice, who was brimming with her own excitement. She had accepted the job in Ethiopia and had decided to stop in Egypt on her way to Addis Ababa. A conference of nonaligned countries would be meeting in Cairo. By adding a little money to my pre-paid ticket I could meet her there after I left Venice. The prospect of seeing Joe and Bahnti Williamson again was exhilarating. The Liberian couple had been brother and sister to me during my stay in Egypt. David Du Bois, the son of Shirley Graham and stepson of Dr. Du Bois, also lived in Cairo and we had been very close friends. A visit to Cairo sounded like the real answer to the malaise which had descended around me. When I learned that Julian and Ana Livia were also going to attend the Cairo conference, it was clear that I would accept Bernstein's offer and re-arrange my ticket to stop in Egypt on my return to Ghana.

I took delight from the flicker of worry which crossed Guy's face. I had told him that I was leaving for Germany and Italy and Egypt. He recovered too soon to please me.

"Have a wonderful time, Mom. A wonderful time."

Since the Ghanaian pound could not be exchanged on the international market, I swapped my cash with a friend for his Nigerian pounds and packed my new flamboyant African clothes and my gifts of gold jewelry. I was going to meet a group of sophisticated New York actors, some of whom were my friends, and I meant to strut.

I became nervous only when I thought of the years since I had been on the stage. (Playing *Mother Courage* in Ghana's National Theatre didn't really count.) The other actors, all brilliant and ferociously ambitious, had moved around New York City's theatres, competing with professionals and growing with each role. Their names and work had become known and lauded. I decided to spend two days in Frankfurt, boning up on the play, or those actors would run me off the stage.

The trip on Lufthansa was a test in discomfort. The flight stewards spoke excellent English and were solicitous without being intrusive, but I kept my eyes on the script in my lap, and let my mind wander from the German accents to John Hersey's book *The Wall* which had gripped me with horror in my youth. I listened to the speech of the passengers returning to their fatherland and remembered the black and white photographs of emaciated human beings rescued from Auschwitz. It was distressing. In Ghana I worked hard at forgiving those African chiefs who collaborated in the slave trade centuries before, but couldn't find it in my heart to exonerate the stewardesses who were toddlers at the time of the Holocaust. Prejudice is a burden which confuses the past, threatens the future, and renders the present inaccessible.

I rehearsed in a small pension in Frankfurt until the lines came automatically to my mind and my tongue. I had learned years before that if I was to act in a play it was wise to memorize every part, even the scenes in which I did not appear. The resulting confidence would spill over into my own role.

Berlin, with its cold temperature, its high-rises, wide, clean avenues and White, White people was exactly what I wanted to see and where I needed to be. I began to relax even as I was being driven from the airport to the Hilton Hotel. When I arrived at my destination I found wide, carpeted corridors, a large, well-furnished bedroom and a bathroom white as a Protestant heaven.

I thought of some Africans I had met who so loved the glories of Europe, they were too immobilized to construct a splendid African future.

This was easy to understand. Europe had ruled long, had brought to Africa a language, a religion, modern ideas of medicine, and its own pervading self-love. How could one suggest in one's own secret heart that Whites were not gods, descending from heaven, and like gods, bringing bounty on one hand and brutality on the other? That was the way of the gods.

After a bath, I dressed in my most glorious pale lavender silk Grand Bou Bou, and went down to meet the cast.

Raymond St. Jacques was still so handsome he looked as if he had been sculpted, then cast in copper. Cecily Tyson was smaller than I remembered and much more glamorous. We embraced and laughed at finding ourselves, of all places, in Germany. Godfrey Cambridge had been unable to come to Berlin because he was in a Broadway show, but Lex Monson and Jay Flash Riley pulled me off the floor with their embraces, and the young Lou Gossett, one half legs and the other smiles, bounced up and down to see me. James Earl Jones and I exchanged our customary cool salutes. Years before in New York City we had worked successfully creating a distance which time had not narrowed.

"Lady! Ah, my Lady!" A sonorous voice completed the welcome I had been seeking. Roscoe Lee Browne entered the rehearsal room and I nearly shouted. He had lost none of his princely air nor elegant good looks. He laughed outright when he saw me, and he spoke to me as he spoke to all women; as if we were Fairie Queens.

We embraced and walked away from the cast and began to tell each other of our current lives. We went to a bar and ordered drinks. Roscoe had heard rumors of my recent divorce, and was genuinely sorry to find that they were founded on fact. He asked about my acceptance in Ghana, adding that he had known President Nkrumah when they had both studied at Lincoln University.

I had prepared a tale for the cast, which had Africans and Black Americans lovingly striding arm in arm up a golden staircase to an all sepia paradise inhabited with black-robed Black saints strumming on ebony harps. I had no need to lie to Roscoe, who would have seen through the fiction anyway.

"We have it good, very good, or bad. Heartbreakingly bad."

Roscoe made his face long. "Africans find it hard to forgive us slavery, don't they?" He took my hand and said, "I thought you would have known that. My dear, they can't forgive us, and even more terrible, they can't forgive themselves. They're like the young here in this tragic country. They will never forgive their parents for what they did to the Jews, and they can't forgive the Jews for surviving and being a living testament to human bestiality." He patted my hand. "Now, dear lady, tell me the good side—but first let me hear the story you're going to tell everyone else."

He laughed when I said I'd spare him the part about all of the Black Americans climbing aboard a chariot and humming our way to heaven.

He said, "Not unless they cast me as De Lawd." It was wonderful to laugh again, and particularly sweet to laugh Black American rueful laughter in Germany.

*The Blacks* translated into German became *Die Negers*. Posters were on bold display throughout Berlin which made the cast snicker behind Black hands. Lex said, "It's a good thing they're speaking German. The first American cracker that comes up to me and says 'I saw you in *de Niggers'* is going to get a nigger beating that'll make him do a million novenas." That was particularly funny coming from Monson who played the Catholic priest in the play, coached the actors in church liturgy and whose youth as a devoted acolyte still influenced his adult mannerisms.

Helen Martin, who had the role of the Black Queen and whose sharp tongue was an instrument to be avoided, said, "I hope these Germans don't think they're getting away with something. We know who they are and what they're saying. I hope I don't have to read them the real Riot Act before it's finished."

I listened and participated in the sardonic responses and realized again the difference between the Black American and the African. Over centuries of oppression we had developed a doctrine of resistance which included false docility and sarcasm. We also had a most un-African trait: we were nearly always ready and willing to fight. Too frequently we fought among ourselves, rendering our neighborhoods dangerous to traverse. But Whites knew that our bellicosity could disperse into other places, on jobs, in elevators, on buses, and in social gatherings.

Single White men seldom physically threatened single Black men, saying "You know they will cut you."

An ancient joke among Blacks told of a bigot who was chided by his friends for calling all Blacks "niggers."

"But that's what they are," he announced.

"What do you call the minister of the venerable White Rock Baptist Church?"

The bigot answered, "A nigger."

"And the president of the Black university?"

"A nigger."

"And the award-winning scientist?"

"A nigger," was the reply.

"And that Black man standing over there watching us with a knife in his hand?"

"Oh, I call him, 'Sir.' "

Black American insouciance was the one missing element in West Africa. Courtesy and form, traditional dignity, respectful dismissal and history were the apparent ropes holding their society close and nearly impenetrable. But my people had been unable to guard against intrusions of any sort, so we had developed audacious defenses which lay just under the skin. At any moment they might seep through the pores and show themselves without regard to propriety, manners or even physical safety. I had missed those thrilling attitudes, without being aware of their absence.

Rehearsals went smoothly. The actors were unselfconscious and professional. An uninformed observer would have been flabbergasted at the difference between the rehearsal cast who moved with an easy grace through the staging and the same cast which burst onto the stage opening night.

Throughout practice each of us had concentrated on our lines and movements, noticing our colleagues for physical and spoken cues, but on the afternoon before opening, the usual excitement was heightened by Jay Flash Riley who lighted the tinder for a group explosion.

Jay, in his outlandish military costume, and wearing the caricatured mask of a White colonial soldier, popped his head in each dressing room and speaking in an exaggerated guttural accent said, "Remember Jesse Owens!" We all laughed, but we all remembered. In Germany, during the 1936 Olympics, the Black runner, Owens, representing the United States, had won four gold medals and shattered Adolf Hitler's dictum that the Aryan race was superior. The German audience reportedly booed

Owens, and Hitler refused to allow the winner to accept the medal from his hands.

There was no mention of Jay's statement, but we left our dressing rooms determined to show the Germans that while we were only eight people, we were serious actors and angry Blacks, and we could call the entire Allied army back and put it onto the stage, and whip them one more time.

After numerous bravos and standing ovations, we attended a reception in the theatre's modern gleaming lobby. The strain of opening night and my efforts to hold my own with those actors exhausted me, and I was tired to the point of perversity.

A blond, trim man with two women approached me and gave a neat little bow. "Madame Angelou, you are a great artist." He told me his name was Dieter, and added that he was an architect. "I want to introduce my wife and mother. We would like to invite you to supper."

He presented the women who complimented me in dainty English.

"It is our honor, Madame."

"Our country is uplifted by your visit."

They looked like three dolls from a porcelain collection.

"We would like you and any friends of yours to come to an après-theatre club. There is a jazz orchestra."

Irascibility prompted me. I said, "I am too tired tonight, but I'd love to come to your house tomorrow. I've never been in a German home." Surprise at my request held their attention for brief seconds. Then the women looked at the man, who nodded. "That will be possible, Madame. We will prepare breakfast. I will pick you up here at 10:00 A.M. Please feel free to ask anyone you like." He handed me his card and I shook hands with the

women. The man kissed the air above my hand and saluted me with a discreet click of his heels.

"Until tomorrow, Madame."

Roscoe had left the reception early, and I didn't think
any other actors would be amused to see strange Germans
en famille. A young and very handsome Jewish man
wearing a yarmulke was standing alone by a bar. I went to
him and began a conversation. His name was Torvash,
and he was an Israeli actor on tour, and had enjoyed our
performance. I asked about Arik Lavy, a Sabra singer I
had known years earlier in Tel Aviv. The actor knew him.
He laughed easily and was pleasant to talk with. I relaxed
and told him of my invitation, adding that I certainly was
expected to bring along another Black from the cast. He
looked at me sharply, "You're not inviting me, I hope?"

That must have been in intention from the moment I
saw his yarmulke, but I said nothing.

"To a German home? I do not mean to be rude, but
why do you think they invited you?"

"They really asked me to a night club. They planned to
make a grand entrance. When Black people are scarce,
we're in style." His laugh was quick and pretty.

"Did you tell them you would ask me?"

"I hadn't seen you then."

He thought a minute. "I'll come along. It should be interesting."

We shared a drink, agreed on the time to meet and
bade each other a good night.

I slept poorly, unable to shake the feeling that I had
forced an invitation, then taken advantage of it. An act,
not criminal, but not quite savory.

I awakened with the Fifty-first Psalm reciting itself in
my head. "Have mercy upon me, O God, according to

Thy loving kindness; according to the multitude of Thy tender mercies, blot out mine transgressions."

As I prepared for the morning's appointment, I assured myself that the situation could not possibly end negatively. We were after all, decades away from Germany's evil days, and if my host, my escort and I weren't good people, at least we were sophisticated.

I put on a bib of filigree gold and a grand bou bou of lace, whiter than ice, and went down to meet my host. He stood in the middle of the glass and chrome lobby talking to a child. The merry-go-round of people spinning near him did not draw his attention. The boy, a miniature color drawing of Dieter, and dressed like him in pressed pants, blue worsted jacket, white open-neck shirt and ascot, was admiring his surroundings. I didn't really want to interrupt their conversation, but I said, "Good morning."

"Oh, Madame Angelou." He appeared pleased to see me.

"May I present my son, Hans?" The child, who was about ten, stiffened, said in heavily accented English, "How do you do?" bowed and clicked his little heels.

Oh Lord, I had lucked upon a right one. I did what any or most of my people do when they really have no alternative, I laughed.

"Madame Angelou, have you friends coming, too?"

"Well, not a friend exactly, but I met an Israeli actor last night and since we were both alone, I invited him to escort me to breakfast." There was only a slight focusing of his eyes on me, which was followed by a gracious smile.

"Wonderful. I suppose you met Torvash. I saw him here last night. He is a very popular comedian-mime. He tours

Europe each year and it's nearly impossible to get tickets to his concerts. Oh, here he is now."

Torvash arrived quickly as if spun off the eddy of people. We shook hands. The two men greeted each other. Little Hans bowed when he was introduced, and suddenly we were both forgotten. The two men swept into a German conversation. I imagined their words probing like dentists' picks. Their eyes were darting, searching.

The boy and I followed the men to a car parked in the driveway, and when the back door was opened for us by a doorman I made no protest, although I expected to be offered a seat up front. After all, I was the invited guest, but the men claimed each other's attention so thoroughly, small graces went begging.

They talked until Dieter stopped the car beside a large, very modern two-story house. We descended and walked on pavement among shaped shrubs and entered the house from the side door, and Hans rushed up the stairs.

Dieter shouted to his wife and led us downstairs. I sent Torvash a few suggestive looks, but he didn't respond.

The basement was a huge dining room dominated by an oversize round table which was set with silver, napkins and glasses. When I looked away from the table, I saw full bouquets of cut flowers in crystal vases on small tables, in the empty and dust-free fireplace and in corners. A screened double door led to a rear garden.

Dieter's wife was giving the room last minute domestic attention. She stopped to shake my hand and welcome me then stepped past me and extended her hand to Torvash. I watched her face tense then relax in less than a second, and we were given seats at the table. Dieter said he was going to bring beer, and his wife excused herself, saying she had to get to the kitchen.

I took advantage of our first moments alone.

"Well, what do you think?"

Torvash shook his head sadly. "He was probably a Nazi. That's what I think."

We might have come from the same small southern town, or urban ghetto or East European village. I shook my head and clicked my tongue. He imitated the gesture and made a bitter face.

"Do you want to leave?" I was ready to walk out with him.

"No. We will see this to the end. I understand you asking me, I don't understand why he asked you." At that moment the entire family entered carrying trays of food.

Dieter set bottles of beer in the table's center, his wife placed whole loaves of bread and large mounds of butter on a side buffet. Hans brought a tray of sausages and went back through the door bringing a roasted ham. Dieter's mother-in-law came smiling, and set potato salad in front of Torvash.

"Good morning, this is for you." She spoke in German, and Torvash stood to shake her hand. After I spoke to her she centered her concern on her Israeli guest. The night before she had appeared to be a contained, conservative, quiet, middle-aged German woman, but she bloomed for Torvash and couldn't stop talking, and giggling, and flirting. She had lost a sense of her age and place.

Dieter interrupted.

"Mother." He smiled, but spoke sternly and she arose, flushing, and left the table.

Dieter said to me, "You see, we didn't know who your guest would be, but it's no problem. We have made arrangements for him."

Torvash said, "Sorry for any inconvenience." Dieter said, "A guest in our home is no inconvenience." His wife smiled and added, "I had salmon all ready." She bobbed her head, "We have one more trip and then we can begin to eat." Again the family trooped out of the room.

I said, "Torvash, you've made a conquest."

He didn't raise his eyes from the table. "Jews are for German women as Blacks are for nice White women in the States. They dream of us, the untouchables, and maybe we dream of them. But we are unsafe, except as toys."

I had seen some White women in the United States flirt so outrageously with Black men in public that they reminded me of dogs in heat. But after rubbing against the men, rolling their eyes and licking their lips, if the Black man asked for dates and persisted, the women would not only refuse, but would become angry that the men were forgetting their manners. It was a cruel minuet danced between spike-heeled women and barefoot men.

The family returned bringing hard boiled eggs, salmon, pickles, mayonnaise, mustards and relish, and I ate without a blessing but with gusto. Dieter must have spoken sharply to his mother-in-law in the kichen, for she never said another word—just kept her eyes on the table, attacking the food angrily.

Between bites we engaged in nerve dulling small talk. I told the listeners where I was from, Torvash listed the cities on his tour, Dieter related in detail the incidents of his visits to the United States, and his wife smiled a lot. Hans and his grandmother ate.

A middle-aged couple came through the garden door and were introduced as neighbors who had been invited to join us for beer.

Their surprise when they were introduced made it obvious that they had expected to meet Die Negers, but not the Jew. Flushed, they sat near Dieter and spoke to me in good but halting English. After another inestimable spate of uninteresting conversation, I asked for a joke.

I said, "I collect jokes. I believe that if you know what a person eats, how and if he prays, how he loves and what makes him laugh, you can claim to understand him, at least a little. I'll tell you a Black American story and you tell me a German one." Immediately I began to recount a Brer Rabbit tale from my childhood which showed the hare defenseless and threatened. As always, in African and Afro-American folktales, the seemingly weak animal with the sharpest brain outwits its well-armed adversary. I left the listeners without a doubt that the vulnerable trickster represented my people and the heavily equipped opponent was the White race. The tale always drew agreeing laughter from Blacks, but the only response I got from that company was a few polite chuckles. We drank more beer and I prodded them for a story.

"Just so I can say I have really met Germans and heard their humor."

The visitors and Dieter spoke to each other, obviously making suggestions which one or the other would reject. Dieter said, "Get Torvash to tell an Israeli joke. He must know millions. He comes from a people known for their black humor." He smiled, "No pun intended." Torvash spoke, looking directly at me. "I do know a story. It's not an Israeli one, nor is it, strictly speaking, a German story, but rather German and Jewish. If that's all right?" The air tightened in the room and there was a barely audible gasp from Dieter's mother-in-law.

I said, "Please tell it. I'm sure everyone wants to hear it."

When I looked at Dieter and his neighbors I knew how wrong I was.

Their faces were stricken with white surprise, but Dieter recovered. He said, "By all means. A German and Jewish story? Do tell it."

Torvash leaned back in his chair and began in a soft voice.

"There was a Jewish man during World War II who had a sixth sense and would have premonitions whenever the Brown Shirts or SS troops were going to make a raid. He would leave the place moments before the soldiers would arrive. It was a gift he had."

I scanned the faces at the table. They had turned mottled grey, like certain Italian marble, and their bodies were held stiffly, not unlike marble statuary.

Torvash continued smoothly as if telling a fairy tale to enchanted children. "The man had gone on like that for three years, but one day his talent deserted him and he was caught."

It seemed that Torvash and I were the only people breathing air. The rest had their lips slightly parted, but there was no visible contracting of their nostrils or chests.

"And the soldiers took the Jew to an SS officer who began to interrogate him. The officer said, 'I know you are the one who has been escaping us all these years. You think you are clever.' " Torvash had straightened up in his chair. His face was suddenly seamless and his eyes were like stones. He had become the Nazi officer. " 'I will see how clever you are. I shall ask you one question. If you answer correctly, I will let you immigrate. If you are wrong . . .' " The actor paused and looked at Dieter. "You know."

I answered, surprising myself by saying, "I know. Go on."

Torvash resumed his performance as the German. "One

of my eyes is false. It was made for me by the world's greatest false eye maker. It cost me a fortune. If you can look at my eyes and tell which one is false, you will be allowed to leave Germany."

Then the actor's shoulders slumped and pulled forward, his face lengthened and began to shake, his eyes opened in fear and his lips were suddenly loose. He was the terrified Jew in the clutch of fear.

"I know, sir, I know. I know because the false one looks so human."

Torvash dropped the old man's face as if it had been a mask and said, "My father, who survived, said that was a popular story in his concentration camp."

It seemed to me that no one moved, or coughed, or even breathed. I know that the story had fallen from my ears, down into my chest, and I found it hard to fill my lungs.

Dieter recovered first. "Yes, I have heard that one myself. Now," he rose, "if I could have some help we will have dessert."

He refused his neighbor's offer to help clear the table. "No, just family. You stay and entertain our guests." Dieter's wife, her face free of emotion, began to remove plates and silverware with remarkable efficiency. In moments, Torvash, the neighbors and I were seated before a table which showed no evidence of ever having been used.

"I wish you had not told that story." The neighbor's voice was just above a whisper. His wife nodded, her mouth grim. "Yes, you see Dieter has a false eye, but you couldn't know that."

The family trooped noisily back to the table smiling and bringing fruit, bowls of whipped cream, tarts, cheeses and more beer. To my surprise they seemed at ease, as if in leaving the room for a few minutes they had obliterated their own awful history.

Dieter sat down and handed out dessert while his wife poured coffee into ornate, yet fragile cups.

We all murmured appreciation for the beautifully presented sweets and the abundance of the meal. I refused to examine Dieter's eyes. When each plate was laden and the last coffee poured, Dieter leaned back into his chair and spoke, "We have a story. A German folktale." The pronoun hinted at collusion, and I looked at Torvash who kept a placid face.

"This story is very old and most German children hear it before they reach their teens."

Despite the obliqueness or childishness of a folk-tale, I knew it could be used to serve the teller's end. Apprehension stirred on my neck and arms.

Dieter's face was rosy with anticipation. "Ready? Shall I tell it?" Everyone, including Torvash, agreed. I settled back hoping to enjoy the story.

Dieter coughed and began, "Once a German worker was on his way to the factory. It was a bitter, cold morning, and the worker was hurrying along when he saw a small bird on the ground, too cold to move. The worker picked up the bird and felt a small heart beat. He held the bird cupped in his hands and breathed hard, blowing warm air on the little bird."

He mimicked the action, his face shining with concentration. "And because of the schnapps he had just drunk with coffee and the warm breath, the bird began to liven, to stir. The worker repeated blowing and blowing and the little bird opened both eyes. But just then, the factory bell rang. The worker was puzzled. What could he do? He had to get to the factory, but he couldn't put the bird back down to finish freezing to death. He looked around, and a cow had just passed and left a large pat on the ground. Steam was rising from the pat. The worker said, 'Oh, that's what I will do.' So he walked over and pushed the little bird down into the hot pat of cow dung, and went to work. That is the end of act one."

I looked at the company and saw all the faces beaming except that of my escort, whose skin was the color of tallow.

"The second act finds the bird recovered. He sticks his head up and out of the dung and loudly, very loudly begins to peep. 'Peep, peep, peep.' That's the end of the second act. Third act: A wolf in the forest has hunted for days for food and found nothing. He is starving. He hears 'peep, peep, peep,' and walks to the pat of cow dung, and sees the bird and opens his mouth, and gobbles the bird down like this."

Dieter spreads his mouth open and shows how the wolf swallowed the bird.

"And that is the end of the third act, and the end of the story, except that there are three morals. One . . ." Dieter turns just a little to face Torvash, "Remember, he who puts you in the shit is not necessarily your enemy. And two, he who takes you out is not necessarily your friend." Dieter stood from his chair and leaned his back against the wall. "And the most important moral of all is . . ." He raised his voice into a shout, "Once you find yourself in the shit, keep your big mouth shut."

Everything began to swell at once. My heart was too full of blood, and the blood was pounding too fast in my ears. The people at the table were suddenly huge, white papier mâché-like unpainted figures in a Mexican parade. Torvash became all Jews, and it seemed the necktie he wore was strangling him. The odors of fresh strawberries and burnt sugar mixed with the smell of beer and sausages. I almost toppled over the table as I ran for the door.

The garden was as neat as a living room, and I searched for a covert corner to vomit up all the hate I had just ingested. I hung over a row of yellow flowers willing to drown them in bile, but nothing came except a salty hot water that I dribbled into the asters.

When I returned to the room, the people were sitting in their same chairs and speaking German softly. Dieter stood as I approached the table. "Oh, my dear Mrs. Angelou, I suppose your constitution is not used to such a heavy German breakfast. Do you feel better now?"

The SS officer and the Jew, the bird, the pile of cow dung, and the starving wolf had disappeared. The two men were like champion boxers who, having delivered smashing blows, had returned to their corners for relief. Dieter was again the solicitous host and Torvash had his normal look of bemusement. The others were calm.

"I'd like to go to my hotel. Thank you for everything."

"Oh, but I must show you my collection of African art."

"Really, I'm not feeling well. I must—" I nodded to the visitors and to Dieter's wife. "Sorry, but I must."

"Then we will leave through the other way. You can see some of the art on the way out. Are you ready?" Torvash shook hands around the room and we went up the few stairs to a side door through which we had entered. Dieter said, "Come this way," and we followed.

The white walls on either side of the hall were crowded with African masks. Dieter described them as we passed. "This is Bambara, this is Fon. Here are Yoruba burial urns. This is Ashanti. I have a large collection of Ashanti gold weights in the other room. If you'd like to see . . ."

I mumbled, "Not this time. I must take my medicine every four hours." The lie came so unexpectedly even I believed it.

"Well, the next time you come to Berlin ..." He pointed, "Here are some Benin bronzes on that wall."

We had reached the front door, so I opened it and walked out into the sunshine.

We sat in the car. I was again in the back seat. Dieter turned his torso around to speak to me. "Since you live in Ghana, I thought you might like to do some trade for me. Of course I have an agent here in Berlin, but his prices are very high and I am certain the Africans don't see even one percent of that money. Maybe you could do something for me."

"I don't trade. I particularly don't trade in African art."

Torvash turned slightly, his light eyes glowing amber and his lips pulled into a smile.

Dieter said, "I am a serious collector, and if you could get some old Ashanti carvings and maybe some Bambara for me or masks from Sierra Leone ... I'd pay you very well. Very well."

I didn't need to look at Torvash, I was certain that his smile was widening.

"I don't trade, Dieter, and I'd really like to get to my hotel."

There was little conversation, only some muttering from the front seat which I ignored. I sat trying to hold my mind together, trying to keep it blank.

At the hotel Dieter was still polite. He bowed over my hand and thanked me for a superb morning. He and Torvash shook hands. They were like two acquaintances who had shared a taxi. There was no admittance that each had walked uninvited into the other's most private place, and shone a painful light.

Dieter drove away and I turned to the Israeli. "I'm sorry. I started something I didn't expect."

"At least we know why you were invited."

I nodded. "He wanted me to exploit the African sculptors. I didn't expect that."

"I think you should examine your reason for accepting the invitation." Torvash took my hand. "Neither you nor I can afford to be so innocent. Not here in Germany or anywhere in this world, unless we admit that we want the return of slavery and the concentration camps." He gave me a sad smile and walked away down the street.

I told only Roscoe about the incident. He said, "Excellent stories. Exceptional and expectable. But you are the most interesting element of the tale. The Israeli knew, and you should have known what would happen. Be careful, dear girl, that Africa doesn't take away all your cynicism. You have become dangerously young."

The play's exquisite writing gathered me and the actors into itself, and we, becharmed, did its bidding without protest. The script vilified all Whites, and we used each opportunity to shout profanities at the German audience which accepted each calumny as if they either didn't comprehend our meanings, or thought of our diatribes as the insignificant mouthings of insignificant clowns.

I wondered how well another play with other actors would have fared. Would the audience have stood and thrown roses if the actors had been Jewish, re-enacting a scene in Dachau? I knew the answer and I disliked the Germans for pandering to us, and I disliked myself and the cast for being bullies.

When I realized that I wanted to apologize to my friends, all Jews and even the Germans, I knew that Africa had creolized me. I was neither meat nor fowl nor good red herring. My native sassiness which had brought me from under the heels of brutes, had been softened by contact with the respectfulness of Ghanaians, yet, unlike them

I did not belong to a place from which I could not be dislodged. I had put on just learned airs along with my African cloth, and paraded, pretending to an exotic foreign poise I had not earned nor directly inherited.

In the actors' company I laughed or shook my head or grunted because I knew the cues and sounds necessary for acceptance, but I had become something other, another kind of person. The New York actors were concerned with what plays were going into production, what roles were going to be filled, and how on earth or on any other planet could a Black actor, talented and trained, exact success from a resistance race and a difficult profession. They were quick and pretty and clever, and when the brief tour concluded they would return home where their restless striving would be not only understood, but expected. The European trip had simply taken them from the arena for a brief respite, but even as they rested they honed their reflexes and practiced their footwork.

We left Berlin for Italy, without regret or hesitation. The actors were looking forward to yet another stage, and I was eager to see Venice again.

Once we arrived in the city of canals, I learned that we were to perform in the lush Teatro La Fenice. I remembered the first time I had seen the jewel box of a theatre.

Ten years earlier when *Porgy and Bess* had played there and Venice was the first European city I had ever seen, I walked its narrow streets and created a fictional connection between myself and its past. I had been a lover of a doge, a sister to Othello and Correggio's generous patron. For a short while I let my Black American history sink beneath the surface of the city's sluggish water. All the citizens of Venice had been our friends. Gondoliers on the

Grand Canal had saluted us with arias from the opera and children followed the cast singing their heavily accented version of "Summertime."

The surface of Venice had not changed. The same birds flew their same swooping patterns over the same tourists in the unchanging San Marco Square. But when "The Blacks" arrived in the floating city, some citizens, angered by the worldliness of presentations at the Venice Biennale, had taken their protests to the streets. As we prepared to enter the theatre we met angry people shouting, "We do not want your filth in Venice." Our Italian sponsors shrugged their shoulders and told us the demonstrators were religious fanatics and we should ignore them.

Some of my colleagues were disposed to follow that advice, but I found it hard to pretend indifference.

Raymond and Lex saw my nervousness and assured me that I had nothing to worry about.

Raymond said, "Queenie, if they touch one hair on your natural, they'll sing 'O Sole Mio' in another key and out of another hole. Come on, let's go!" We put our heads up and marched in as if the Pope had given us the pretty little theatre just because we were so righteous.

The audience applauded Genet and the audacious cast. The next few days passed without particular interest. My thoughts had turned to Egypt. I was about to walk on the streets where a good marriage went bad, and sit in parlors where my ex-husband and I had worn veiled but angry looks.

There were no last minute tearful departures among me and the cast. Everything we had had to share had been exchanged. Their eyes were filled with excitement for the next play, or for Hollywood, for success which was waiting for them to claim it. Roscoe saw me to the launch which was the first leg of my journey to Cairo. At the wharf he held me, then pulled away.

"Be careful, sweet lady. You went to Africa to get something, but remember you did not go empty handed. Don't lose what you had to get something which just may not work. And I have heard, 'If it don't fit, don't force it.' Bad grammar, but sound advice." In honor of his wisdom, he raised one eyebrow and I raised two. There was nothing to add, so we embraced and left each other with a laugh.

From the airplane window sunlight on the Sahara made the sandscape look like a lumpy butterscotch ocean.

The Williamsons sent their limousine to collect me from the Cairo airport. Two of their children accompanied the driver. Although Baby Joe and Edwina, four and six years old, had grown up from infancy in Egypt with Arabic nannies and Egyptian children, they still had the manners and even the accents of the children I had come to know in Ghana. They greeted me with hugs, then sat dignified in the car seats, waiting for me to begin the conversation. They responded to my questions directly and briefly.

Yes, their parents were well. Yes, they were enjoying school. Yes, they had lots of friends. Yes, their Arabic was good. Edwina, suddenly excited, asked, "Auntie Maya, do you know the Old Man is here?"

Liberians affectionately called their president, William V. S. Tubman, "Old Man." Edwina told me that he was "very good and smokes more cigars than Daddy and they are bigger, too." Baby Joe explained, "But he is the President." Once they had broken the mold of proper childish behavior, they would not put it together again. They chattered about parties and punishments, and what friends were visiting from Liberia. I was told that Edwina was reading well, and I had to listen to Baby Joe say his ABC's. They spoke about their mother's pregnancy with a charming naturalness. Baby Joe wanted another sister. "Edwina can be not good, you know." Liberians rarely accuse a person of being overtly bad, but they use the opprobrium of being "not good."

I arrived at the residency. Bahnti Williamson was waiting. "Ooh, Auntie Maya, welcome home."

She smiled, showed a pretty set of small, white teeth, and stretched her arms to me. "Ooh, Auntie Maya, how we have been anxious to see you. Ooh, Auntie." She turned her baby-filled belly to the side so that we could embrace, and I felt at home.

During the nearly two years when I had lived in Cairo with a teenage son I scarcely understood, and a husband I understood too well, Bahnti and her husband Joe, Jarra and Kebidetch Mesfin, an Ethiopian couple, and David Du Bois, had given me their laughter, love, company and very little advice.

Bahnti and I entered the residency, which had the air of a Liberian village during feast day. Henry, the Williamsons' oldest son, Bahnti's younger sister, cousins, Liberian visitors and wives of African diplomats stationed in Cairo crowded around embracing me and shaking my hand. After we sat together eating "country chop" (a spicy African stew) and toasted my arrival, Bahnti took me to a guest room where she explained that Joe was almost too busy to come home.

The president had brought a large retinue of cabinet members to attend the conference of nonaligned countries, and Joe, as Liberian Ambassador, had to be available to the delegation every minute. She said that she had hardly been able to await my arrival. There was no one to help in the preparations for the president's visit to the residency, which would take place in two days. I allowed myself to forget the twenty or more relatives, friends and servants who hovered over her like drone bees around the queen, preening her and making her comfortable.

"Sister, Ooh Auntie Maya, if you hadn't come, I would never receive the 'Old Man.'" African and southern Black American women can exude a charm which acts as a narcotic on their targets. The living room had seemed perfect when I entered, but if Bahnti asked me, I was willing to repaint, hang new wallpaper or simply move the furniture.

We sat on her balcony at sunset with frosty drinks. Bahnti told plain stories with such humorous embellishment that I would choke on laughter. Each time a spasm would shake my body, Bahnti would throw her hands in the air and say, "Oh Sister Maya, oh Auntie, you are the funny one. Old Man say in my country laughter is better than rice. Now Sister, you must listen. Joe has told President Tubman about you, and he has promised that you will sing for him day after tomorrow night."

I choked again, "What? Sing? Sing what?"

"Oh, but Auntie, you know Old Man studied in the states and he loves the Negro Spirituals. Auntie, you used to sing them to us and the children. So Old Man is expecting to sing 'Swing Low, Sweet Chariot' with you."

I drank and considered the request. There was no chance that I would refuse it, but at least I wanted Bahnti to know that what she was asking of me was not a small thing.

Many years had passed since I had sung in night clubs for a living, and although I had had moderate success I never had illusions about my musical or vocal talents. I succeeded because I wore exotic costumes and told interesting stories against a musical background.

I said, "Sister Alzetta." Calling her by her given name was one way to let her know how seriously I regarded her request. "I hope you have not led the president to think I am a Miriam Makeba. She is a singer, I just sometimes carry the tune."

My statement must have also tickled the unborn baby, because Bahnti held her stomach as she laughed. "Oh Auntie, Old Man knows how great Miss Makeba is, but he can't fold up his tongue to sing those click songs. He's going to sing 'Swing Low, Sweet Chariot' with you just as he learned it in the South of America. Not in South Africa. Hoo, hoo."

I explained that I was going to meet Black American friends from Ghana who were attending the conference.

Her laughter still echoed in my mind as I was driven by her chauffeur to the Cairo Hilton. Julian, Alice and I sat in the air-conditioned restaurant ordering hot dogs, hamburgers and french fries. Ana Livia had joined colleagues from her country who formed the Puerto Rican Delegation of Petitioners. Julian, as a member of the Ghana Press Delegation, had sat in on a few of the nonaligned conference meetings, and he was full of news.

As soon as I could break into his speech, I told them of

my assignment to sing with President Tubman and how nervous I was. Their laughter rivaled Bahnti's.

Julian recovered first. "So, Maya Angelou, you've made it all the way from Arkansas to Africa so that you can perform for a president? You couldn't get to the White House so you aimed for the Black House. Okay, I'm proud of you."

Alice said Liberia had been settled by freed American slaves, and their descendants still formed the elite so maybe I was related to the president. There was no reason to be nervous. I should just consider that maybe I was singing at a family reunion.

I went with them to meet David, who was in his usual state of overcommitment. He worked as a journalist at the Egyptian News Service as well as a stringer for international news services.

After a hearty and genial greeting, we began a garrulous chatter of conversation which sense would hardly penetrate. David spoke glowingly of Malcolm X's recent visit to Cairo, and wanted to know what we could do to protect him when he returned. Alice announced that she had taken the E.C.A. job in Addis Ababa, and asked who did we know in Ethiopia. I wanted suggestions for my presidential command performance. Julian wanted to hear about the conference, the conferees, and every detail of their plans.

None of us really expected the other to respond to our statements. It was enough to make the pronouncements and ask the questions in a friendly atmosphere. We knew that ultimately, each of us would be obliged to carry out our own assignments and find our own solutions. The brief gathering was nurturing and when the commotion abated we parted quite satisfied.

The Liberian Residency was festooned with flags and

garlands. The family and family friends waited impa-
tiently. Servants wearing new clothes and rehearsed into
numbness stood at military attention in the foyer, and the
children, quieted by the importance of the occasion,
formed their own small line inside the salon.

Beyond the open door, along the steps and down the
walk to the entry gatehouse, Egyptian and Liberian soldiers, their weapons at the ready, awaited President Tubman. The unnatural and uncomfortable silence was
broken by the arrival of cars and the shouted orders of
Army officers. Joe left the family rank and descended the
stairs to meet a group of beribboned and laughing men.

William V. S. Tubman was surrounded by his court of
cabinet ministers, but he was clearly visible, and after the
phalanx had climbed the stairs, he entered the building
arm in arm with Ambassador Williamson. Although he
wore a tuxedo heavily adorned with medals and ribbons,
he looked like an ordinary man that one might meet in
church or in the Elks Hall or in any Black American community. That impression was short-lived—for after he
embraced Bahnti and the other family members, Joe presented me. "Mr. President, this is our friend, the American singer Maya Angelou." The force of the man was
befuddling. I didn't know whether to bob or curtsy.

"Oh, Miss Angelou, I have been looking forward to this
evening. To have some of A. B.'s good Liberian chop and
some Negro spirituals. Welcome." He and his energy
passed me and I felt as if a light had been turned off. He
was a president with a royal aura.

People born into democracies and who have learned to
repeat, if not to practice, the statement that all men are
created equal think themselves immune to the power of
monarchies. They are pridefully certain that they would
never tug their forelocks nor would their knees ever bend

to a lord, laird or feudal master. But most have never had those beliefs put to test. Being physically close to extreme power causes one to experience a giddiness, an intoxication.

At that moment, I wanted to be close to President Tubman's aura, encompassed by, warmed, and held forever in its rich embrace.

At formal dinner, I was seated far away from the important officials, but close enough to observe them entertaining their leader. Each person had a story, told in the unique Liberian accent, and as each story concluded, President Tubman approved the telling by adding an appropriate proverb for each tale. The cabinet ministers and diplomats beamed with pride and laughed easily with and for their "Old Man."

When dinner was finished, Joe led the guests into the decorated salon. As President Tubman sat in a thronelike chair flanked by his suddenly serious attendants, Bahnti looked at me and raised her eyebrows. Joe introduced me, saying although I was a singer and writer, much more important I was the auntie of his children, a daughter of Africa and his chosen sister.

"Mr. President, excuse me." I was standing in the center of the salon. "I have never sung for a president. In fact, I've never met a president before."

William Tubman laughed and rolled his giant cigar between his fingers. "My child," he chuckled and his retinue chuckled, "My child, I am just a common garden variety president. Sing!" I began a traditional blues in a comfortable tempo. The president snapped his fingers and the guests slowly followed his example. When I finished the song the applause was loud and long.

"Now, my child, sing 'Swing Low, Sweet Chariot.'"

I began the old song, softly. "Swing Low, Sweet Chariot, Coming for to carry me home." The president's baritone joined. "Swing Low, Sweet Chariot, Coming for to carry me home."

Other voices picked a harmonic path into the song, and I heard Bahnti's high soprano waver, "If you get there before I do, Coming for to carry me home, Tell all my friends I'm coming too, Coming for to carry me home." They sounded neither like Whites nor like Black Americans, but they sang with such emotion that tears filled my eyes. Save for a few Egyptian government officials and me, all the singers were African. I knew from the dinner conversation that not one of them was fired with religious zeal, so for what chariot were they calling and what home could they possibly miss? I dropped my voice and gave them the song.

They were Americo-Liberians. Possibly five generations before, an ancestor—an American slave—had immigrated to Africa to marry into one of the local tribes. Now, after a century of intermarriage, they sat in beribboned tuxedos in this formal salon, drinking French champagne, models of the international diplomatic community. In their own land they owned rubber plantations and rice and coffee farms, and in their homes they spoke Bassa and Kru and Mandinke and Vai as easily as they spoke English.

Still, their faces glowed as they picked up the melody.

> See that host all dressed in red,
> Coming for to carry me home.
> It looks like a band that Moses led,
> Coming for to carry me home.

They were earnest and their voices were in tune, but they could not duplicate the haunting melody of our singing. While it is true that not all Black Americans can sing or dance, those who do create tones so unique that they are immediately identifiable. Of all Africans I had heard, only the Zulus, Xhosas, and Shonas of South Africa produced the velvet and wistful sounds which were capable of reaching the ear and heart with an undeniable message of pain.

Did it mean that only the African, and only the African living in total despair, pressed down by fate, refused, rejected and abandoned could develop and sing this kind of music?

The strains faded away and beautiful smiles accompanied the audience's applause. In the absence of my creative ancestors who picked that melody out of cotton sacks, I humbly bowed my head.

When Guy met me at the airport with chocolates (expensive) and a lovely piece of African cloth which he himself had chosen at the market, I was quick to think that my absence had made his heart grow fonder. His face was young with trust again, and he was laughing again—hearty, open laughter. I concluded that my decision to stay as long as possible with Bahnti and Joe had been wise, for my son had come back from that adolescent region where the barriers were so dense and high, they kept out prying eyes and even light.

He carried my bags into the house and the aroma of fried chicken met me at the door. I knew that dish was beyond Otu's talent and since Alice and Vicki were gone . . . I looked questioningly at Guy.

He smiled and hugged me. "I cooked it, Mom. I know you hate airplane food."

The tears on my face surprised me and distressed Guy. We had not used weeping to manipulate each other. I apologized and Guy said, "Maybe this is not the time to talk to you."

I insisted that the time to talk was when one had something to say. I sat, still in my traveling clothes, while Guy spoke as carefully as if he was reading a prepared treatise.

He declared his gratitude for all I had ever done. He announced that I was an excellent mother. He said no parent could have been more patient, more generous or more loving. I began to contract, to tighten my muscles and my mind for the blow which I knew was coming. Because it was not a wallop, it slipped up on and into me like a whisper.

"Mom," he looked like the sweet boy I had such joy raising. "Mom, I've thought about this seriously and continuously since you left. You have finished mothering a child. You did a very good job. Now, I am a man. Your life is your own, and mine belongs to me. I am not rejecting you, I'm just explaining that our relationship has changed. . . ."

He was not pulling at the apron strings, he was carefully and methodically untying the knots and raveling the very thread.

"I have not decided just what I want to do. Whether I shall stay in Ghana and finish at the university, or go to another country to finish my education. In any case, I shall apply for scholarship so you can be free of the burden of my tuition."

Now the entire apron was a pile of lint and I was speechless. He talked, beckoning me into his thoughts, but I was unable to follow him. I didn't know the road.

At the end of his speech, he hugged me again and thanked me again, and saying he had plans for dinner, went out the door.

I walked around the empty house trying to make sense of the sentences which tumbled over themselves in my brain.

"He's gone. My lovely little boy is gone and will never return. That big confident strange man has done away with my little boy, and he has the gall to say he loves me. How can he love me? He doesn't know me, and I sure as hell don't know him."

Efua appeared at my door, drawn, her usual healthy skin the color of gun metal. When she entered the house I saw her trembling hands. I knew better than to ask any questions. At the proper time she would say why she had come to me.

When I returned from the kitchen with cool beer, she was more composed but she was still standing in the middle of the living room.

"Sister, have you seen it? Have you seen the paper?" I said no, and wondered if the president had been assassinated. I implored her to sit, but she shook her head.

"Today's paper. Second page."

A presidential assassination would have claimed front page.

"Sister Efua, please come, and sit and let me pour you beer."

She remained erect, but shaking, oblivious to my entreaties.

"No one has claimed him. No one has come. Oh my Africa! What is happening to you? Oh my Africa."

The dramatic cries overwhelmed my suddenly very small living room. She could have filled a Greek theatre stage.

"Oh my Africa! Where are you going?"

I poured a glass of beer for her and placed it on a table beside a chair. I took mine to another seat and waited.

"Oh. Oh. My country. My people."

The moans began to fade and Efua finally came aware of her location. She gave me a wan smile. "Sister, excuse me, but I suppose you might not understand. A man, an Ashanti, a Ghanaian died two days ago. His body was lain in the morgue. No one has come for him."

She had her gaze on me, but the vacant eyes were staring and I was not being recorded in her vision.

"Do you know what that means?"

I shook my head.

"Africa is breaking. That body in the morgue is a stone from Africa's mountain. He belongs someplace. The day he was given a name he was also given a place which no one but he himself can fill. And after his death, that place remains his, although he has gone to the country of the dead. His family and clan will honor his possession of that place and cherish him. Never in Ghana has a body lain unclaimed for two days. That is why the newspaper has reported it. It should have been on the front page. Headlines. Africans must be shocked into realizing what is happening to them. To us."

She shook her head and gathering her cloth around her shoulders, walked through the doorway. I followed. She stood on my porch, turning her head slowly, looking from left to right to left at the houses and cars in my street. When she spoke her voice was low, nearly a moan. "Everybody in these cities should be made to go live in his native village for one year, barefoot and in rags. We have begun to think like Europeans. Sister, mind you, our gods will become angry. I would be afraid to anger Jesus Christ, but I confess, the thought of angering African gods absolutely terrifies me."

She leaned to kiss me farewell and walked down to her car where the chauffeur stood holding the door for her.

The visit muddled me. Efua, the model of containment, had been weeping not over the death of a stranger, but because other people who were also strangers had not come for his remains. As usual, as if I had been sent to the continent on assignment, I placed the African and Black American cultures side by side for examination. In Ghana, one unclaimed corpse merited principal news coverage, and Efua's emotional response, while in America, Black bodies still quick with life demanded no such concern. Too often among ourselves, since lives were cheap, dying was cheaper. Since the end of slavery, Black Americans running or walking, hitchhiking or hoboing from untenable place to unsupportable place, had died in fields, in prisons, hospitals, on battlegrounds, in beds and barns, and if pain accompanied their births, only the dying knew of their deaths. They had come and gone unrecorded save in symbolic lore, and unclaimed save by the soil which turned them into earth again.

I thought of the African gods whom Efua was loath to anger and decided that they must have been bristling with rage for centuries. How else explain the alliance of African greed and European infamy which built a slave stealing-selling industry lasting for over three centuries? Weren't the African gods showing their anger when they allowed the strongest daughters and sons to be carried beyond the seas' horizon? How much had they been provoked to permit disease and droughts and malnutrition to lay clouds of misery on the land? I agreed with Efua. I certainly would not like to see the gods of Africa anymore riled up than they were already.

The evening paper reported the family had come from the north to collect the body. Ghanaians breathed more easily, and so did I.

Misery is a faithful company keeper, and Comfort was dissolving under its attention. I watched for three months as her laughter diminished then disappeared along with about thirty pounds of sensuous curves. There was no jollity in her face, nor was there any strength in her hands.

When she strung my hair, the movement on my head could have been caused by two sleepy snails going to rest.

"No, Sistah, I am not sick. Just weary."

We had come to know each other well enough for me to use an admonishing tone. "Sister, you have wearied yourself into bad health. You're so weak now you can hardly pull the comb through my hair."

Months before she would have blamed my hair, saying that it had a mind of its own and I should have the impertinence beaten out of it.

She said only, "I am getting weaker each day." She paused, then said, "It's the woman. She's doing it."

I asked, "What woman? Doing what?"

Even Comfort's voice was being erased. She said in a whisper, "His old wife is using some bad medicine on me. First she gave permission for us to be friendly, then when she saw how he loves me, she said 'no.' "

"Friendly? Comfort, did she think you would be just friends with her man? Plain friends?"

"She knew we were loving. Why else would my mother speak to her mother? And she agreed. Then . . . and then she saw that we were more than loving. We were . . . he liked me. That's when she promised I would lose. Lose everything. My looks, my weight. I would lose him and my mind. Oh, Sistah, she has power medicine. I might even lose my life."

"Did she give you something to drink?" I thought of arsenic.

"No, I eat at home. I have a cousin and a servant from my village who look after me. No. I have taken nothing that she has touched." She pulled a stool and sat beside me. I remarked that she looked like a little girl.

She said, "Sistah, I feel old, but I think she is taking old age from me."

Had she talked to the woman herself? Maybe if she went to the woman . . .

Comfort began to shudder and I apologized for the suggestion. She waved a bony hand at me.

"No, Sistah Maya, now you see my trouble?" She shivered and her eyes were filled with despair.

"The woman came to me. To my house. My steward let her in. Sistah, I went in to her. I was surprised. She is old. Once she looked fine, but now . . . Oh age . . . I will not live to see what it can do to me." She was near to tears, so I encouraged her to continue with her story.

"Well, Sistah, you know I was fat and fine as cocoa butter, and the man was loving me. Anyway, when she came to my house I asked her what she wanted . . . not sweetly, and she said she wanted to ask me two questions. God forgive me, but I was crazy. I didn't offer her a drink. I wouldn't even sit down. She is old, Sistah, and I still stood looking down on her." Comfort shook her head, wanting not to believe her own rudeness. She continued.

"She was wearing an old mourning cloth; she said, 'My first question is, do you know what love costs?' And I told her," Comfort crossed her hands atop her head, "I am not a market woman, so I do not think of everything in money terms. Then she said, 'My last question is, are you ready to pay anything for love?' A spell must have been on me then, because I lost all my training. I talked. I raised my voice. I said I wasn't so old and ugly I had to buy love, and I felt sorry for anybody who had to do so.

"Then I made my biggest mistake, because she stood up and said, 'You feel sorry for the person who bought love? Is that true?' She was looking at my mouth, and I laughed and chipsed. Sistah, I sucked my teeth at that woman. Even I can't believe I did that. The old woman wrapped her mourning cloth tight around her and said, 'You will lose. You will lose all,' and then she walked out of my house. Oooh, and Sistah, see me now? The man will not come to me. My flesh is falling away. Do your people have medicine? Power medicine?"

I asked her if she had seen a doctor, and she shook her head, "European doctors have nothing to help my condition. Don't you Black Americans have medicine?"

Many Black-owned newspapers in the United States carried announcements in the classified sections of magic practitioners.

> Get your man back!
> High John the Conqueror Roots

No one I knew admitted to using their services.

I had to tell Comfort that my people had no reliable medicine except that they had learned in school.

She said she had been to many African doctors and found no one able to move the terrible curse. She had even spent a week in Larteh, a town which hosts hundreds of practitioners, but had had no success. Her last hope was to travel to another country.

"Sistah, I have heard of a woman in Sierra Leone. She is very very good. I must go and stay two weeks, cleansing myself, and then she will see me. I must pay her in pure gold."

I said, "I don't have gold, but let me lend you some money."

Weakness made her old, robust smile gentle, "Sistah, thank you, but my uncle is a goldsmith, and I have plenty of trinkets. What I want is to go and come. I want us to sit out in your compound on a Saturday. I want my strength back so that when I put my hands on your head you will know that Comfort has her hands on your head, and I want you to make me laugh. Oh Sistah, I cannot say how much I want to laugh."

We embraced when she left and she promised to see me again in two months. Fine, fat and laughing.

Two weeks later a friend of Comfort's came to my door. "Sister Maya, I have come with very sad news. Our Sister, Comfort, died in Sierra Leone. She had not been there a week. Sorry to bring this news, but I knew you would want to know. She so loved to laugh with you."

Malcolm was a prompt and exciting correspondent, using the mails to inform, instruct, and encourage us. His letters were weighty with news and rich in details of his daily life. The United States was on the brink of making great changes, and the time was ripe for the Organization of Afro-American Unity. His family was wonderful and it just might be increasing. Death threats were proliferating in his post box and he changed his telephone number frequently to protect his wife from vulgar and frightening callers.

Some of his letters were plain directives:

A young painter named Tom Feelings is coming to Ghana. Do everything you can for him. I am counting on you.

The U.S. State Department is sending James Farmer to Ghana. The Ambassador will pick out special people for him to see and special places he should go. I want you all to collect him and show him around. Treat him as you treated me. I am counting on you.

There were good people working for the OAAU, full of energy and enthusiasm, but none had the organizational skills to set up and run an efficient office. What they needed was an experienced coordinator.

He didn't mention that I had worked as Northern Coordinator for Martin Luther King's SCLC. By omitting the reminder, he forced me to speculate upon my possible value to the organization. I went to Julian for advice. He said, "I suspect we'll all be home soon. Africa was here when we arrived and it's not going anywhere. You can always come back."

Alice's letter from Ethiopia pushed me closer to my decision. She wrote that Malcolm came through Addis, looking good but harried and still traveling without a companion. "If he gets that OAAU in shape, he'd be sure to have people around him. Like you and Julian, I'm worried for his safety."

My Ghanaian friends said they would be sorry to see me go, but they understood that my people's struggle came first.

I thought long and carefully before I came to a final decision.

My son convinced me, and had nearly succeeded in convincing himself, that he was a grown man. He was either doing brilliant work at the university or, when he was distracted, none at all. He was a character in a drama

of his own composition, and was living the plot as it un-
folded. Even if he forgot his lines, his mannishness
wouldn't allow him to accept prompting.

When I told him I was thinking of returning to the
United States, he had smiled broadly.

"Yes, Mom. It is time for you to go back home."

His only frown came when I said I would pay up his
tuition and leave him a solid bank account.

"I'm really sorry I have to take your money, Mother,
but someday ... someday." Visions of future affluence
danced in his eyes. The little boy and even the rambunctious teenager had strutted upon the stage and exited.
This new leading man did not need a mother as support-
ing actress in his scene. He welcomed having the stage to
himself at last.

It seemed that I had gotten all Africa had to give me. I
had met people and made friends. Efua, Kwesi Brew, T.
D. Bafoo and Nana had woven themselves as important
strands into the fabric of my life. I had gotten to know and
love the children of Africa, from Baby Joe to the clever
Kojo, the bouncing Abena, the grave Ralph and the lady-
like Esi Rieter. They had given me their affection and in-
structed me on the positive power of literally knowing
one's place. Sheikhali had provided African romance, and
Comfort's life and her death had proved the reality of
African illusion. Alice and Vicki and Julian and Ana
Livia would return to the United States someday and we
would stir up our cauldron of old love and old arguments,
and not one whit of steam would have been lost during
our separation. I had seen the African moon grow red as
fire over the black hills at Aburi and listened to African
priests implore God in rhythm and voices which carried
me back to Calvary Baptist Church in San Francisco.

If the heart of Africa still remained allusive, my search for it had brought me closer to understanding myself and other human beings. The ache for home lives in all of us, the safe place where we can go as we are and not be questioned. It impels mighty ambitions and dangerous capers. We amass great fortunes at the cost of our souls, or risk our lives in drug dens from London's Soho, to San Francisco's Haight-Ashbury. We shout in Baptist churches, wear yarmulkes and wigs and argue even the tiniest points in the Torah, or worship the sun and refuse to kill cows for the starving. Hoping that by doing these things, home will find us acceptable or failing that, that we will forget our awful yearning for it.

My mind was made up. I would go back to the United States as soon as possible.

Nana Nketsia was traveling to Lagos by car and when he invited me and his two oldest daughters to accompany him as far as the Togo border, I accepted gratefully. Now that I had decided to leave Africa, I realized I had not seen Eastern Ghana.

Araba rode with me and Adae got into her father's car. Three hours after we left Accra we arrived at the small but busy town of Aflao. Nana beckoned me to follow and led me to a large two-story stone house at the end of a quiet lane.

"We will stay here for the night, and at dawn my driver and I will continue to Lagos. Come inside, I want you to meet our host, the customs officer." A servant responded to Nana's knock and his daughters, Nana and I were shown into a daintily furnished sitting room. Before we could choose seats a young girl around Araba's age entered through a side door. She smiled and extended her hands and made a little curtsy to Nana.

"Nana, welcome. I am Freida, Adadevo's daughter. He is still at the office. I will make you comfortable."

Nana introduced Araba, Adae and me, and Freida bobbed prettily, accepting the introduction. She supposed we would be weary after such a long journey and offered to show us to our rooms. Nana was put on the ground floor, and I was given a second floor guest room. Araba and Adae were to share a room near Freida.

Although I was used to the dignity of African girls, I was taken aback by Freida's grown-up composure at sixteen. She was a practiced hostess. I surmised that she was an only child of a single parent and circumstances had forced her to grow up quickly and very well. Nana carried his shortwave radio to his quarters and I retired to my room.

For the next hours as the girls giggled down the hall, I thought of my impending departure and the Organization of Afro American Unity. There had been no mention of salary or responsibilities. I knew that I would be paid the minimal wage and would be asked to raise money, organize files, recruit members, stuff envelopes, draft news releases, type, file and answer the telephone.

Those were the usual chores that go begging in understaffed and underfinanced civil rights organizations.

It would be good to see my family and old friends. Suddenly I was excited at the prospect of being back in New York City, and back in the fray.

Araba broke into my thoughts. "Auntie Maya, Mr. Adadevo is here, and dinner is served." I prepared myself and joined the group in the dining room.

Mr. Adadevo was a tall, dark brown man of pleasing appearance, and when he spoke his voice sang with the melodic Ewe accent. The girls sat together at dinner, using English to talk across their language barrier while Nana and Mr. Adadevo spoke of portentous matters of State. The hours of assessment in the guest room had drained my energy, and I was glad there was no general conversation which could command my participation.

At an early hour, I asked to be excused, honestly claiming exhaustion.

The bed, sleep and I met together and I rose at dawn to go downstairs and bid Nana a safe journey. He promised that he would return to Ghana before my departure.

When Mr. Adadevo entered the kitchen the day was bright and I was having yet another cup of instant coffee. He ate quartered oranges and asked me why I was only then visiting his area. I made a courteous reply, then he asked if I would like to see the nearby town of Keta only thirty miles away. Without any real interest I again answered courteously.

"That would be nice. We should start back to Accra by early afternoon." He assured me that we would have plenty of time and left to rouse the still sleeping girls.

It was decided that we would take his large car. Araba, Adae and Freida sat in the back, and Mr. Adadevo, his driver and I occupied the front seat.

The countryside was beautiful, but not unusually so. My eyes had become accustomed to coconut trees and palms, and bougainvillaea growing freely on country roads and city streets. A quiet murmur reached me from the back seat and since neither Mr. Adadevo nor his driver spoke, I was lulled by the car motor and the moist warm air into a near torpor.

Suddenly, I jerked alert and looked ahead. We were approaching a sturdy and graceful bridge. My heart began to race and I was struggling for breath. I gasped, "Stop, stop the car. Stop the car." The driver consented. I was sitting next to the window, so I opened the door and quickly stepped to the ground. I spoke through the back window.

"Get out, girls. Come. You, too, Freida. We are going to walk across this bridge." Although they were stunned by my behavior, they obeyed, and I said to the startled Adadevo, "We will join the car on the other side." I walked briskly apart from my charges who were unsettled by my actions and tittering nervously. My pretended concern over the waterscape and the overgrown river banks caused me to turn my head often, as if looking for a particular object or view. In fact, I was more jittery than the teenagers. I could not explain my behavior. I only knew that the possibility of riding across that bridge so terrified me that had the driver refused to stop, I would have jumped from the still moving car.

Mr. Adadevo was standing at the end of the bridge, and after he saw the passengers safely in the back seat, he took my arm and drew me aside.

"Why were you afraid? I have rarely seen such terror. Do you know anything about this bridge?" I shook my head.

"Have you ever heard of the Keta bridge?" I shook my

head again. I had never heard the area mentioned. "The old bridge, I should say bridges," his face was solemn, "were infamous for being so poorly constructed that in any flood they would crumble and wash away. People in conveyances of any kind lost their lives, so a century ago passengers in palanquins used to stop and get down in order to walk across. In a crisis, only people on foot could hope to reach the other side." I felt a quick chill. He asked, "Are you sure someone didn't tell you that story?" I said, "I must have read it somewhere." I apologized for startling him and knew without question that I had no inkling of the bridge's history.

After my inexplicable outburst, there was a new tension in the car. No sounds came from the back seat, but Mr. Adadevo began speaking immediately after the bridge episode and didn't stop until we reached Keta.

He talked about Accra, of Ghana's growth, of the wisdom of Kwame Nkrumah. He said he admired the American Negro athletes and Dr. Martin Luther King. He spoke of his region, describing it in detail, its fishing and copra industries, its markets and major towns, and its religion.

I half heard his crooned chant as I was more engrossed in examining my actions at the bridge.

"There is a lagoon behind Keta and of course the ocean before it, and that has caused the people of the town a great problem. For after the work of enlarging the ports of Tema and Sekondi-Takowadi, the ocean has reacted by backing up onto Keta. They have already lost over two miles of the town. The people are being squeezed by two forces of water. The town will disappear in time and the people have nowhere to go."

When I heard the dire story, I again surprised myself. I

felt as if I had just been told a beloved relative was dying. Tears came to my eyes and threatened to run down my face. I dreaded the possibility of crying before strangers, but even more awful was the prospect of allowing Nana's daughters to see me out of control. The motto of their family was "royalty does not weep in the street," and I had spent a great effort showing them that although I was born from slaves, I was descended from kings.

I took a handkerchief and faked a cough.

Araba leaned foward, "Auntie, are you all right?"

I told her I thought I was reacting to the dust, and she was satisfied.

Adae, asserting her intelligence and explaining me to her new friend, said "Auntie is very sensitive. She has allergies." I was grateful for their presence, for without them I might have bent over my lap and let the emotion of loss drain out of me in rivers of tears. I swallowed the knots in my throat over and over and wondered if I was losing my mind. What did that bridge and the sea's encroachment on Keta have to do with me?

Adadevo was still talking as the car turned through the narrow streets of the old town. Although we could not see the ocean, suddenly I knew or felt that the next turn would give us a panoramic view of the surf. I held onto myself and hoped that the presentiment would prove false.

Mr. Adadevo said, "Now here is the sea. You call it the Atlantic Ocean. We have another name for it in Ewe."

The driver parked at the side of Keta's market and Mr. Adadevo asked me to come and meet his sister, who had a stall on the market's periphery. We walked in file with Freida and the driver carrying large empty straw baskets.

Mr. Adadevo's sister was tall and thin and resembled

Efua. When we were introduced, I found that she spoke very scanty English and I expected that she would speak French.

The Ewe tribe which occupied Togo and the eastern area of Ghana had been a German colony in the nineteenth century, but after Germany's loss of World War I, the allied victors took away Germany's mandate and gave the area to France. French became the province's official language in 1920, so I offered to speak French with my host's sister, but her French was only a little better than her English. We smiled at each other and shook our heads in exasperation. She spoke rapid Ewe with her brother and niece, while Araba and Adae looked on.

I waved good-bye, anxious to climb into the raised market which was issuing sounds of trade and merriment.

The narrow stairs were bounded by wooden walls, making the entrance dim. I was looking down, making certain of my footfall, when a voice above me drew my attention. I looked up to see an older woman, unusually tall, blotting out the light behind her. She spoke again and in a voice somewhat similar to my own, but I was unable to understand her.

I smiled and, using Fanti, said regretfully, "I am sorry, Auntie, but I don't speak Ewe." She put her hands on her wide hips, reared back and let loose into the dim close air around us a tirade of angry words. When she stopped, I offered, in French and in a self-deprecating tone, "I am sorry, Auntie, but I don't speak Ewe."

She clapped her hands close enough to my face for me to feel the rush of air, then she raised her voice. My ignorance of the meaning of her words did not prevent me from knowing that I was being denounced in the strongest possible language.

When I could wedge myself into her explosion, I spoke in English nearly whining, "Auntie, I am sorry, but I do not speak Ewe."

It seemed the walls would collapse. The big woman took a step down to me, and I backed down two steps. There was no room on the stairs for me to pass her, and I wouldn't have had the nerve to try to force my way beyond that now enraged giant frame. Her invective was coming faster and louder. I knew that my luck had to have totally deserted me to allow me to meet a mad woman on darkened stairs who I could neither placate nor threaten.

Mr. Adadevo spoke behind me, and I turned only slightly, afraid to leave my back unprotected.

"Mr. Adadevo, would you please talk to this Auntie. I can't make her understand."

The woman fired another salvo, and Mr. Adadevo stepped up and placed himself between me and my assailant. He spoke softly in Ewe. I heard the word "American" while I was watching the woman's face. She shook her head in denial. My protector spoke again, still softly. I heard "American Negro." Still the woman's face showed disbelief.

Mr. Adadevo looked at me and said, "Sister, she thinks you are someone else. Do you have your American passport with you?"

I hadn't seen my passport in two years, but I remembered having an old California driver's license, which had its identifying photograph. I took the wrinkled, but still slick paper from my wallet and gave it to Mr. Adadevo. He handed the document to the woman who strained to see in the darkness. She turned and walked up the stairs into the light. Mr. Adadevo followed and I followed him.

There, the woman, who was over six feet tall, stood peering at the flimsy piece of paper in her dark hand. When she raised her head, I nearly fell back down the steps: she had the wide face and slanted eyes of my grandmother. Her lips were large and beautifully shaped like my grandmother's, and her cheek bones were high like those of my grandmother. The woman solemnly returned the license to Mr. Adadevo who gave it back to me, then the woman reached out and touched my shoulder hesitantly. She softly patted my cheek a few times. Her face had changed. Outrage had given way to melancholia. After a few seconds of studying me, the woman lifted both arms and lacing her fingers together clasped her hands and put them on the top of her head. She rocked a little from side to side and issued a pitiful little moan.

In Arkansas, when I was a child, if my brother or I put our hands on our heads as the woman before me was doing, my grandmother would stop in her work and come to remove our hands and warn us that the gesture brought bad luck.

Mr. Adadevo spoke to me quietly, "That's the way we mourn."

The woman let her arms fall and stepping up to me, spoke and took my hand, pulling me gently away. Mr. Adadevo said, "She wants you to go with her. We will follow." The girls and the driver had climbed the stairs and we entered the crowded market. I allowed myself to be tugged forward by the big woman who was a little taller than I and twice my size.

She stopped at the first stall and addressed a woman who must have been the proprietor. In the spate of words, I heard "American Negro." The woman looked at me disbelieving and came around the corner of her counter to have a better look. She shook her head and, lifting her arms, placed her hands on her head, rocking from side to side.

My companions were standing just behind me as the vendor leaned over the shelf where tomatoes, onions, and peppers were arranged in an artistic display. She began speaking, and raking the produce toward the edge.

Mr. Adadevo said something to the driver who came forward and placed each vegetable carefully into his basket. My host said, "She is giving this to you. She says she has more if you want it."

I went to the woman to thank her, but as I approached she looked at me and groaned, and cried, and put her hands on her head. The big woman was crying too. Their distress was contagious, and my lack of understanding made it especially so. I wanted to apologize, but I didn't know what I would ask pardon for.

I turned to Mr. Adadevo and asked if they thought I looked like someone who had died.

He answered and his voice was sad, "The first woman thought you were the daughter of a friend. But now you remind them of someone, but not anyone they knew personally."

My guide now pulled me through a press of bodies until we came to a stall where the owner sold yams, cassava and other tubers. Her wares were stacked on the ground in front of the stall and rose in piles around the stool she occupied. My escort began her litany to the saleswoman. Somewhere in the ritual she said "American Negro" and the woman repeated the first stall owner's behavior. Freida began putting yams and cocoa yams and cassava into her basket. The two women were rocking and moaning.

I said, "Mr. Adadevo, you must tell me what's happening."

He said, "This is a very sad story and I can't tell it all or tell it well." I waited while he looked around. He began again, "During the slavery period Keta was a good sized village. It was hit very hard by the slave trade. Very hard. In fact, at one point every inhabitant was either killed or taken. The only escapees were children who ran away and hid in the bush. Many of them watched from their hiding places as their parents were beaten and put into chains. They saw the slaves set fire to the village. They saw mothers and fathers take infants by their feet and bash their heads against tree trunks rather than see them sold into slavery. What they saw they remembered and all that they remembered they told over and over.

"The children were taken in by nearby villagers and grew to maturity. They married and had children and rebuilt Keta. They told the tale to their offspring. These women are the descendants of those orphaned children. They have heard the stories often, and the deeds are still as fresh as if they happened during their lifetimes. And you, Sister, you look so much like them, even the tone of your voice is like theirs. They are sure you are descended from those stolen mothers and fathers. That is why they mourn. Not for you but for their lost people."

A sadness descended on me, simultaneously somber and wonderful. I had not consciously come to Ghana to find the roots of my beginnings, but I had continually and accidentally tripped over them or fallen upon them in my everyday life. Once I had been taken for Bambara, and cared for by other Africans as they would care for a Bambara woman. Nana's family of Ahantas claimed me, crediting my resemblance to a relative as proof of my Ahanta background. And here in my last days in Africa, descendants of a pillaged past saw their history in my face and heard their ancestors speak through my voice.

The first woman continued leading me from stall to stall, introducing me. Each time the merchant would disbelieve the statement that I was an American Negro, and each time she would gasp and mourn, moan and offer me her goods.

The women wept and I wept. I too cried for the lost people, their ancestors and mine. But I was also weeping with a curious joy. Despite the murders, rapes and suicides, we had survived. The middle passage and the auction block had not erased us. Not humiliations nor lynchings, individual cruelties nor collective oppression had been able to eradicate us from the earth. We had come through despite our own ignorance and gullibility, and the ignorance and rapacious greed of our assailants.

There was much to cry for, much to mourn, but in my heart I felt exalted knowing there was much to celebrate. Although separated from our languages, our families and customs, we had dared to continue to live. We had crossed the unknowable oceans in chains and had written its mystery into "Deep River, my home is over Jordan." Through the centuries of despair and dislocation, we had been creative, because we faced down death by daring to hope.

A few days later at Accra's airport I was surrounded by family and friends. Guy stood, looking like a young lord of summer, straight, sure among his Ghanaian companions. Kwesi Brew, T. D. Bafoo and their wives were there to bid me farewell. Efua and her children, Nana's brood of six, Grace Nuamah and other colleagues from Legon, Sheikhali and Mamali, and some Nigerian acquaintances milled through the crowd. Julian hugged me, "Be strong, girl. Be very strong." Nana's car appeared on the tarmac, and coming through a private door he joined the well-wishers. I drank with each party, and gave and received generous embraces, but I was not sad departing Ghana.

Many years earlier I, or rather someone very like me and certainly related to me, had been taken from Africa by force. This second leave-taking would not be so onerous, for now I knew my people had never completely left Africa. We had sung it in our blues, shouted it in our gospel and danced the continent in our breakdowns. As we carried it to Philadelphia, Boston and Birmingham we had changed its color, modified its rhythms, yet it was Africa which rode in the bulges of our high calves, shook in our protruding behinds and crackled in our wide open laughter.

I could nearly hear the old ones chuckling.

# ABOUT THE AUTHOR

MAYA ANGELOU, author of the best-selling *I Know Why the Caged Bird Sings, Gather Together in My Name, Singin' and Swingin' and Gettin' Merry Like Christmas* and *The Heart of a Woman*, has also written four collections of poetry, *Just Give Me a Cool Drink of Water 'fore I Diiie, Oh Pray My Wings Are Gonna Fit Me Well, And Still I Rise*, and *Shaker Why Don't You Sing?* In theatre, she produced, directed and starred in *Cabaret for Freedom*, in collaboration with Godfrey Cambridge, at New York's Village Gate; starred in Genet's *The Blacks* at the St. Mark's Playhouse and adapted Sophocles' *Ajax*, which premiered at the Mark Taper Forum in Los Angeles in 1974. In film and television, Maya Angelou wrote the original screenplay and musical score for the film *Georgia, Georgia*, wrote and produced a ten-part TV series on African traditions in American life and participated as a guest interviewer for the Public Broadcasting System program *Assignment America.* Her renowned autobiographical accounting of her youth, *I Know Why the Caged Bird Sings*, was aired as a two-hour TV special for CBS in April 1979. Other television accomplishments are the five-part miniseries, *Three Way Choice*, on CBS, for which she was author and executive producer. For PBS she has hosted a study course filmed in thirty half-hour segments, Humanities Through the Arts. In the sixties, at the request of Dr. Martin Luther King, Jr., she became the Northern Coordinator for the Southern Christian Leadership Conference, and in 1975 she received the Ladies' Home Journal "Woman of the Year Award" in Communications. She has received numerous honorary degrees, and has lectured at the major American universities. She received the Golden Eagle Award for her documentary, *Afro-American in the Arts*, for PBS in 1977. She was appointed by President Gerald Ford to the Bicentennial Commission, and by President Jimmy Carter to the Commission of International Women's Year and is on the Board of Trustees of the American Film Institute. One of the few women members of the Directors Guild, Maya Angelou is author of the television screenplays *I Know Why the Caged Bird Sings* and *The Sisters.* In December 1981, she was appointed the first Reynolds Professor of American Studies at Wake Forest University, a life-time appointment.

In 1983, she received the Matrix Award in the field of books from Women in Communications, Inc.